MW01295424

BELIEVE IN FAITH

BELIEVE IN FAITH

THE POWER OF CHRIST IN YOU

MARCUS JOHNSON

To order additional copies of this book, contact:
Xlibris Corporation
1-888-795-4274
www.Xlibris.com
Orders@Xlibris.com
131939

CONTENTS

Prologue

Have you ever once considered writing a book? As I travel throughout various places, people ask me what inspired me to become an author. As I have told my story to many, there have always been those who have said they could never envision themselves writing a book. I must admit that writing a book can be a long process; however, it is not as difficult as many may assume. If you pray to God and ask Him to lead you forward, you will be set on the right path to begin writing your book. I ask that you sit down and think heavily about specific things that you are passionate of to a great extent. Once you pick a topic, identify four or five or more distinct ideas about your topic. Each of the ideas that you develop will consist of a chapter in your book. For example, let us say that I want to write a book on Italian food. Your ideas (chapters) would be things such as the history of Italian food, different kinds of Italian food, different places where you could purchase it, how to prepare it for eating, and the health effects of it. You would also include an introduction (prologue), acknowledgements (people you admire), and a conclusion (epilogue). If you advance by this pattern in writing your book, it would be fairly simple and successful.

I have always found great joy in writing because it is a great opportunity for me to transfer all of God's wisdom within me onto paper. The best part about it is knowing that the entire world can now read and take in the things that God has stored inside of me. I became an author at the young age of fifteen, which was not intended directly. I had written over a total of nine speeches during a course of three months in the beginning of 2009. It was just recent upon a developed interest in politics and world affairs. My goal was to present these speeches throughout the world in an effort to encourage everyone to come together to solve challenges for the future. In the end, those speeches would be published in what would become my first book to ever be written *The Advancement of Common Humanity*. Of course I would be compelled spiritually and by my parents to write and publish additional books, such as *The Call of Destiny: A Liberation from Apathy, Shame, and Failure*.

My underlying goal in writing this book is to define clearly how the life of each and every person can be built upon a strong spiritual foundation under God. I define what it means to have a relationship with Jesus Christ and, more importantly, what it means to have ultimate faith in Him. It is through these principles that you will develop a sense of profound purpose and live a life of greatness. You will learn also how to be the person that God created you to be and why you must do so. All that is written in this book is based solely upon the experiences that I have had throughout my life. I am not writing this because all of the information may be correct. I am writing it because I not only care about people, but I believe in people. I believe in God's ability to turn people's lives around and use them as forces for good.

There are always those who either doubt or deny God's wonderful ability to change their lives for the better. Some people believe that God works only for certain kinds of individuals or specific people, which could not be further from the truth. Each and every person has the opportunity and ability to receive as much of God as they would like. He loves us all, unconditionally, even when we fall short of His glory, which is all the time. The worst sinners of all time still have the chance to be saved and brought closer and closer to the Lord God Jesus Christ. If your life is going down the wrong path, you can get the strength from God to turn onto the right path and lead the life that He has in store for you. You have been given many wonderful things from God to live prosperous and great. He stored these gifts inside of you to perform great deeds in His name. You cannot fulfill any of these deeds without God and His strength. With His strength, you are able to do all of the things He asks of you. When you and I do that of which He asks, He rewards us with not only the ultimate desires of our hearts, but with countless blessings for which we have never asked for and imagined!

Throughout my journey, I have noticed that many of those who proclaim to have a faith in Jesus Christ tend to hold a cynical view upon certain issues, people, and the world itself. They believe that much that is negative do not have the ability to be made positive and much that is wrong in the world do not have the ability to be made right. Many of them believe in secular (spiritually wrong and ungodly) solutions to many of the problems that they face individually and on a broad scale. Many of those without Jesus Christ tend to make excuses and point the blame for much that needs to be fixed. I have developed this conclusion based on those of whom I know very well, what I hear and see in the media and popular culture, and what I see in the public. Someone who does not have Jesus Christ at the forefront of his or her life will most likely base his or her joy and peace on things that bring only temporary joy and satisfaction. Many of these things may consist of alcohol, drugs, money, material items, and the opinion's of others. Some people also put great faith in relationships and friendships, which can be great until things begin to lead down the wrong path. As people continue to do these exact same things again and again, expecting the same result each time, their situation continues to get worse and worse until a breaking point is reached. The worst thing to do is judge an individual based on his or her circumstances and put them down when they do wrong in our eyes. Because of what I have experienced, I am able to understand where certain people are in their lives spiritually. Due to my ultimate faith in Jesus Christ, I am able to help lead others in the right direction, while taking wonderful pleasure in doing so. This is exactly my objective in writing this book.

Before developing my relationship with Jesus Christ, I would ensure my faith in temporary things. I focused more on what I thought may have been wrong with me, and I held a cynical outlook upon myself and my circumstances. After Christ came into my life, I began to learn of and know the very person I am truly. I developed a positive vision of my future and, to this day, I see absolutely nothing short of profound greatness up ahead. More importantly, I gained the strength from God to believe not only in myself, but also in others and the things they can accomplish when they reach out to God on a consistent basis. It has nothing to do with religion by any measure, but with an unwavering commitment to God that begins at the center of your heart. As you read this book, I pray and ask humbly in the name of Jesus Christ that you would consider the following questions inside of your mind:

A) Am I enjoying my life to the fullest?
B) What must I do to develop a deep, committed relationship with Jesus Christ and grow it overtime?
C) Do I have my ultimate faith in the One who created me in His image or in things that bring joy and happiness that is temporary only?
D) Do I know the person that God created me to be?
E) Am I living up truly to God's purpose for my life?
F) How can I grow my faith in Him to the point where I can lead others in the right direction?
G) How can I be the person that God wants me to be in my own life and in the lives of others?
H) How must I realize all of God's wonderful gifts inside of me and use them to make a positive impact upon the world?
I) How can I take my life off of the wrong path and give my life Jesus Christ and change it forever?

I ask that you not only enjoy this book, but let it change you for the better and bring you closer to God than you ever been at any time in your life. After reading it, please be sure and pass it onto someone who needs it.

Introduction

There has never been a day in my life that I am more proud and grateful to be the person I am. I continue to look to the future with hope and confidence in all of the things I aspire to have. During the past six years, so much has taken place that truly shaped my character, my way of thinking, my sense of strength, and my ability to stay focused on the things for which make my life great. I always enjoy thinking about the days when I was much younger when life was all about cartoons, video games, and toys. I re-envision the times when I was little kid waking up in the middle of the night crying. I think sometimes also about the many days in kindergarten and first and second grades when I wanted so badly to return home with my mom. Life was fairly simple and small during these times. There was no need for mentors, or for that matter personal prayer. As I lay my head on my pillow at night reminiscing of the old days, I realize my story will serve as a great source of inspiration for so many individuals across the world.

Upon accepting Jesus Christ into my heart, mind, and soul, I was filled with a profound sense of purpose for achieve greatness for the future. There are days when tears flow down my face like a waterfall because I realize I could have been any other person in any other place at any other time. What has always led me forward was keep faith in Lord Jesus Christ, and I will always be grateful that He changed my life forever. He took a young kid with a world full of potential into a developing young man who has yet to change the world for those to come after. The story you are about to read is the journey God has placed me on, as it will lead me into the wonderful future He has in store. I ask that you put your life aside and envision yourself living the life for which you are about to read.

Chapter 1

A New Beginning

It was in January of 2006 when I was in sixth grade. During this time I was living in Chicago, Illinois at the age of twelve. I was a student at Eugene Field Elementary School in Rogers Park, a neighborhood on the north side in Chicago. Once every year at Eugene Field School there was a spelling bee. A spelling bee was held for each of the grade levels (4th-8th) and one was held for the victors from each grade level bees in a school wide spelling bee. For two consecutive years, one particular won both the grade level and school spelling bees. To each and every other person at Field School, he seemed inevitably strong and undefeatable; however, anything can be possible, and this was proven to be true. I can remember vividly the day when my sixth grade teacher, Mr. Michael Feuer, telling me in low, firm voice, "I need you to win this." I found this incredibly amazing because he told it to me only and no other student. In the classroom competition to determine the two finals to compete in the sixth grade level spelling bee, I won first place and advanced to the next level. On the night before one of the most important days of my entire life, my mom asked me to skip gym class so that I could study the words in the spelling bee. While I was in the classroom studying, some of the other kids were talking about how it was my duty to defeat the current champion. Some of them tested me on the words in the bee.

When we arrived to the auditorium, I saw my mom, which boosted my confidence by one-hundred percent. I was not sure fully and passionate about this competition until I sat down in the chair on stage. It was almost at the end of the competition and only a few of us remained. When the current champion misspelled his word, some in the audience cheered so loudly that they were escorted from the auditorium by school security. It was then only the girl from my classroom and myself left on stage. After she misspelled her word, it was left for me to spell the next word correctly. After I did exactly that, I was declared the sixth grade spelling bee champion. Upon victory, I was advanced to represent the sixth grade in the school wide spelling bee. The winner of the school wide spelling bee would advance then to regional competition. As my class and I were heading to the auditorium for the school spelling bee, I can remember Mr. Feuer calling me off to the side because the former champion wanted to talk to me. He advised me to remain relaxed and take a deep breath before spelling each word. I did exactly as he advised me to do. As before, seeing my mom and dad boosted my confidence by one-hundred percent. Everyone was supporting me during the entire way there, and I realized I had a fundamental stake in pulling off a major victory.

As I was studying the words that were in the competition, I came across the word b*eret* on the list of words. Since I had never seen the word on paper, I assumed the pronunciation of *barret*. If I would have sat in just one chair to my left where one of my opponents sat, I would have spelled *beret* as *burray*, thinking *beret* was *barret*. I still thank God to this very day that this did not happen. It was half through the competition and only two of us remained. My opponent misspelled her word, so it was once again up to me to steal the victory. My final word was *facile*. I struggled for a minute until it came to me instantly. After I spelled *facile* correctly, I was declared the school spelling bee champion and won a shirt and a thirty dollar gift certificate for Barnes & Noble Bookstore. I advanced to the regional level and placed 4th. I was deeply proud of myself for enduring everything I did in accomplishing what so many others have failed to do, which was defeat the two-consecutive year spelling bee champion, who seemed too inevitable to defeat. Most importantly, my family, classmates, and teachers were deeply proud of me for becoming the new school spelling bee winner and champion at Eugene Field Elementary School. After a major victory in the spelling bee, I never thought I would soon join the chess team at school. I previously joined the chess team in fifth grade, but I stopped going to the practices on Monday and Wednesday afternoons. While, talking to my fifth grade teacher, Mr. John Lee, on the phone, I asked him when we could possibly meet again. He told me about a chess tournament that was going to be held at Gale Elementary School. I did not attend with the intention of joining chess team. When I arrived to the tournament, however, I was required to register to be in it. Upon seeing me, my current teacher, Mr. Feuer, was so surprised and glad to see me there. I was never that great of a chess player in contrast to spelling words, and I took responsibility because of so. Sadly, I won one match only out of the five I competed in. The following Tuesday we competed at the citywide chess tournament at the U.S. Cellular Field. In between each match, the other players on our team were showing me various strategies and techniques on the board, but it very little to help me win. Once again, I won one match only out of the total five matches I played at the tournament, which shows I was not that great of a chess player. Even though I was not a very good chess player, I vowed to remain on the chess team and become better until I was a much better player.

Life for me at this time was going very good. I was popular at school, I had a few really good friends, and I predicted many more good comings and achievements.

However, life would soon change . . . . forever! I was sitting in the living room at home with my brother and father. As I was playing video games, I overheard my father tell my brother we were going to move to Louisiana. This decision was a colossal shock to me. All of the times we moved from place to place forced me to adjust to new changes, which was never easy. Even though I really did not want to move to Louisiana, I did not know that life would soon change dramatically. Not only would I have to adjust to the new environment, I would have to brace for a major phase of my life. It was July 11, 2006 when we left Chicago to drive to our new home in Moreauville, Louisiana. Because our electricity was off, we stayed with my auntie for a week. Our electricity was turned on a week later. I woke up the next morning feeling as depressed as ever due to leaving Chicago. Life became a little better after moving into our new home; however, I was still very upset and depressed about moving. A week after moving into our house, we received a call from my auntie in Chicago telling us that my grandmother was probably not going to survive her last stage of cancer. I was very afraid that she would pass away. The next morning, we learned that she passed on because of the cancer she had for quite sometime. My mom and I flew on an airplane to Chicago to attend the funeral service. This gave me the opportunity see my fifth grade teacher and best friend from school, Nicolas Economos. We arrived on a Thursday and remained in our old apartment in which two of my brothers were still living in. At the funeral, which was held on the Wednesday of the following week, at least every person shed tears. My grandfather not only had no enemies, every person in our family loved her very much. A few days after the funeral, my mom and I returned to our new home in Moreauville, Louisiana.

All I could do is complain, be depressed, and pray that all of us would move back to Chicago as soon as I could. I remember having a really bad panic attack in my room due to the entire situation. I was surprised that I did not begin to cut myself because of the way I was feeling. There is no better way to describe things other than to say that life became nothing but pure, living hell. Everything worsened heavily when school began. I learned that my new school did not have many of the activities I enjoyed such as spelling bees, a chess team, or a wrestling team. This made me feel even worse off than before. I was in the principal's office nearly everyday due to being bullied all the time. In the midst of these troubles, I remained heavily focused on my schoolwork and getting the best education. I became an honor roll student easily, I gained the respect and admiration of my teachers, and I did make a few friends and allies. I also won 1st place in the social studies fair and advanced to the regional level. Academically, I was extremely successful as always before. I always stayed focused on my studies and things that mattered the most. Because I was able to, life became a little better so far in Louisiana.

In the beginning of my eighth grade year, I was well-known at school. I transferred soon, however, from Mansura Middle School to the Avoyelles Public

Charter School. I continued to hear so many great things concerning the charter school that I became tempted to offer it a try. The first day I arrived, however, I wanted to return to Mansura Middle School because I did not like very much the environment at the charter school. While the teachers and students were extremely nice and considerate, I still could not adjust myself to the environment so I returned to Mansura Middle School. Life became increasingly better upon returning to Mansura Middle, and I found out from my mom we were moving back to Chicago during the following year. I was no longer overwhelmed with depression, and I was close to profound happiness. However, I would never enter the first ever major triumph of my entire life.

In order to pass the eighth grade, each student was required to pass the LEAP Test, which stands for the Louisiana Educational Assessment Program. All of the students who failed this test would fail the eighth grade, even if they had straight A's. I was so afraid for my life that I would fail this test, thus failing the eighth grade. I began to ask certain people if they thought I would pass the LEAP Test. Every person I asked had told me with no doubt that I was intelligent and smart and that I would pass the test. I still did not have the peace and security within myself about passing the LEAP. However, I was always envisioning myself passing. It was not until March 1st, 2008 that I received the strength from Jesus Christ to believe that I would pass. It was Super Saturday, an activity designed to equip students who desired extra training and practice for the big test. After the activity, my dad and I went to McDonalds. As I was waiting in the parking lot, I said out loud, "Lord Jesus, I am going to pass the LEAP Test with all I have." From that moment forward, I never again felt an ounce of fear of failing. Most importantly, I knew deep within myself that no matter what happens, I would pass the LEAP Test as well as the eighth grade. March 1st, 2008 is also the day when I accepted Jesus Christ into my life, and I will honor this day for as long as I shall ever live.

For the next two months, I withheld the security and assurance concerning my performance on the test. It was on May 6th, 2008 when we received the scores from the LEAP. When the principal called the eighth graders to the cafeteria, we ran so fast that our life could have depended on it. As quickly as everyone wanted his or her scores, none of them could have been as passionate as I was concerning to what I experienced. When each person received an envelope, we were allowed to open them and view our scores. I asked Mr. Allen Warnesdorfer, the principal, if I could step outside to view my scores so I could pray. Mr. Allen knew already whether or not I passed or fail, so he asked me to stand by him and to view my scores for the LEAP Test. After reading the word *passed* on the score paper, I fell to my knees and praised Jesus Christ heavily. I gave Mr. Allen a great hug, and ran to my inclusion teacher's room with tears in my eyes and gave her a giant hug, telling her the good news. After sixth months of doubt, worry, and fear, I accomplished one of the greatest obligations of my life. I passed the LEAP Test and graduated from eighth grade with my fellow classmates as planned.

On March 1st, 2008 at Wal-Mart, I saw one of my old friends from the Avoyelles Public Charter School of whom I had not seen in four months prior to this period. We talked and caught up on how things were going in our lives. She told me she and the rest of the classmates and teachers misses me very much. Upon returning home, she and I became friends on Myspace. We talked to each other quite often on there. On May 19, 2008, however, I found out she deleted and blocked me on Myspace because she thought I was becoming "too serious" with her, even though I had no awareness whatsoever. I began to talk with another one of my best friend. She and I began to communicate often and become close. Sometimes I would call her or just talk to her on the Internet. I began slowly to admire her for more than just a friend. I began soon to feel as if I loved her with all of my heart, and I wanted to marry her some day and start a family. All I could ever think of during the entire summer of 2008 was her. My love for her had grown so strong it began to cause much stress and anxiety. In addition, I desired a license, car, and more independence. At times I felt even as if I desired my own place to live, but I know this was far out of the question. All of these thoughts and desires, including my love for her, bestowed more and more stress and weariness upon me in which I could not handle. I felt deep within my heart that I was going to spend the rest of my life with her; however, on September 9th, 2008, I learned that she felt the exact same way about someone else as I felt about her. This was probably by far the worst day in my entire life at this point. I could not eat a single thing, nor could I concentrate on anything positive. I overcame this downfall a week later. Gracefully, it was another sixteen months before I would have any romantic feelings for any particular girl. This gave me more than enough time to focus on not only schoolwork and getting my education, but many other initiatives that would reach me further in life. I would enter into the next phase of the journey in which God has me upon.

It was August 11th, 2008, the first day of school for me as a freshman in high-school. Before entering high-school, I made a solemn pledge to do as much as possible to achieve excellence and greatness over the next four years. It was sort of a struggle at the beginning of the school year because I was once again in a new school with new people. It did not take long at all to become popular. I joined the clubs of Beta, 4-H, SADD, Fellowship of Christian Students, Drama, Explorer's Club, and the Speech Team. Being a member in all of these clubs at the same time in one school year would have been too much for an average student to handle, I managed fully to handle all of them, while maintaining academic superiority. I ran for president of the SADD Club while I was still a freshman student. In spite of not winning the election, I became great friends with my former opponent. This led to me to building a credibility for myself as a spokesman. I also would become part of something that would soon make a major difference in my life.

I participated in a speech contest that would determinate the finalist to compete at state competition. The contest was being held in the Beta Club. The speech was required to be 3-4 minutes in length; it had to be written by the individual orator, and be memorized fully. In the beginning, it was sort of difficult for me to decide on a topic that I was passionate of, so I chose the importance of getting the best education. As passionate as I stood on education, I felt as if I could not develop the best possible speech on this topic. I decided then to present a speech on the war in Iraq. Since I passionate deeply about political affairs, I knew that a speech on the Iraq war would be fundamentally easily to write and memorize. I worked on the speech for an entire month. I was in and out of the library every single day, editing and correcting errors. All of the people who heard my speech loved it very much, saying that I have a very powerful and firm voice.

While I knew I was great at what I do, most of what I could think about what my opponent was going to do. Some other people told me he was a really good speaker, which was not very pleasing for me to know. I was asking others constantly if the thought I could win, and all of them said yes. This did not help me to stop dwelling on my opponent. A few times I even asked him about his speech, which really had nothing to do with me. As intimidated and stressed as I was, I was soon to learn that my opponent became twice as intimidated by me than I was by him. I can remember the day when I read a poem over the school intercom. I was reading the poem on behalf of the SADD Club, and it emphasized the dangers of tobacco smoke. Much later in the day, I ran into my opponent in the school library. I expected for him to poke fun at me about the poem because he always acted this way towards me. Instead the total opposite had taken place. He told me I did a great job on the poem, so I shook his hand. My opponent told me also that he was going to drop out of the speech competition. I asked him for the reason, which was the lack of desire to continue. However, I knew the real reason that he did not want to continue in the contest. He felt that I was a better speaker than him, and that I would be selected as the finalist to compete at the state convention. There was a previous time when I presented the end of my speech to him. After doing so, he had a depressing look on his face and walked away very fast. The following week after I read the poem, he asked me to present to him my entire speech. My opponent told me that my performance would decide whether or not he would compete against me.

November 3rd, 2008 was the day of the contest in determining the finalist to compete in oratory at the state convention. The ironic element for which happened was learning that my would-be opponent and his brother lived out of the school district. Therefore, the both of them had to transfer to a school in their school district, which made me automatically the finalist to advance to the state convention. I was very glad for this, but not as excited as I would have been if I would have actually defeated my would-be opponent. I was confident fully in my ability to do the best job at the convention. I set my expectation eternally high as to win 1st place at not only the state convention, but the national convention as well. Three days later, however, I was told by my club sponsor of whom I did not like very much that I must write an entirely new speech on an entirely new topic. I was told if I did not write not a new speech that I could not compete in the competition. The reason I had to change the speech was that she did not agree with the stance I supported in my speech. I became so discouraged and disappointed because I worked hard tremendously on my speech and learned it was all for nothing. Two weeks had gone by until I finally developed a new idea for the perfect speech.

It was the day before school ended for Thanksgiving vacation week. I asked some of the other Beta club members about ideas for a speech, which helped a little. I also asked my other club sponsor if I could use the same speech I wrote on the war in Iraq, and she said yes but I would have had to change it to a great extent. I emailed the speech to myself so that I could perfect it on another day. When I arrived home, however, I decided personally to write a new on a different topic. The title of the new speech would be "Unite for Change." In the speech, I would emphasize the fundamental importance for the nation to unite behind President Obama as Democrats and Republicans to solve the nation's challenges. I wrote the speech the following day, and rewrote it the following weekend. When I brought to my club sponsor at school, the both of us worked with and edited it until the convention on January 21st-23rd, 2009. When I presented my new speech to the club members, they enjoyed it as twice as much as the previous one. I felt highly optimistic within myself that I would win 1st Place in oratory at the state convention. I prayed each and every night to Jesus Christ, asking Him to ensure me victory. I envisioned myself being victorious from the beginning to the end; from the state convention to national.

The state convention lasted for two and a half days. Each hotel room was divided with four club members per room. The oratory competition was held on the second day of the trip, which was the first day of the actual convention. I was equipped fully to go in and take what I thought was mine: victory. After presenting my speech, we were allowed to depart from the speaking room. One of the judges approached me in the hallway, gave me a handshake, and told me that I did an excellent job. I was sure that I was victorious after hearing this. After ten to fifteen minutes approximately, a poster with the names of the semi-finalists was posted outside of the speaking room. After seeing that I did not advance into the top twelve, I was disappointed extremely. I was as disappointed as I had been when I found out the girl I loved was in deep love with someone else. Throughout the remaining time of the convention, I could not concentrate on anything but my loss. There came a certain point in which I realized I had no major stake in winning this competition. The reason I felt so disappointed was that I dwelled so much on being victorious that I failed to take every possible measure necessary to win. I also failed to acknowledge there was always the chance God could have something far better in store. I will forever remember this valuable experience because it led to something far much greater and historical.

Upon returning home, I went into the school library and retyped the speech I did for the speech competition. I edited it for four weeks until it would begin to pay off. I presented the speech to two teachers who I was acquainted with greatly. They enjoyed it so much they asked me if I were interested in presenting it to their churches. One of the teachers, Mrs. Mary Smith, arranged for me to give the speech at an African-American history event her church was hosting. The event was held on February 28th, 2009, and this was the day of my first ever public speaking engagement. Everyone enjoyed my speech greatly, telling me afterwards that I would become "another Obama." This was extremely wonderful and inspiring to hear and know. Less than a month later on March 22, 2009, the other teacher who listened to my speech, Mr. George Franklin, arranged for me to speak at his church. Everyone who heard me there enjoyed my speech heavily, telling my father and me that I will achieve great things later in life. I was approached by a man who promised to promote me as a speaker, but it turned out he had no real connections. In spite of this, I began to write more speeches and edit them over time. By the end of June in 2009, I had already completed nine speeches. My intentions were to become promoted as a public speaker, and I had no idea of God's actual intentions.

On May 24th, 2009 I presented a speech that was filmed to be uploaded to Youtube. This would offer me a greater chance to be recognized. I became worried that someone would listen to the speech and steal the material for his or her own personal use. I was talking on the phone with my oldest brother about the situation, and he asked me if I would have liked to publish my speech. He emailed Xlibris Corporation, which is a book publishing company. A publishing consultant called me a couple of days later. I was thinking in my mind that I was going to publish only the speech I had on Youtube, but the remaining eight speeches also . . . . in a book! Publishing this book was very expensive, but it was with full thanks to God through the help of a church that my first book ever was published. *The Advancement of Common Humanity* was published on September 2nd, 2009. After my first book was published, I began immediately thinking of my second book.

It was August 10th, 2009 and school had begun. Most of the kids knew who I was, and I was very popular among many at school. I was respected heavily by all of my teachers. I was a sophomore in high-school and still involved in many extra-curricular activities. I was still involved in SADD, FCS, Speech, Drama/Theater, and Beta. I became involved heavily in the 4-H Club, as it was unexpected. The date was October 20th, 2009. On this day, all of the school 4-H officers met at a youth center to train the elementary students in the club to be strong 4-H leaders. I was the Avoyelles High school 4-H Parliamentarian, so I had to be in attendance. I remember the day before we went when our club sponsor, Mr. Dan Soldani, told us about running for parish wide office. I told myself I was going to prepare my speech campaign speech the following night. It was not until the bus ride to the youth center when I remembered we could run for parish wide office. Our club sponsor asked the club if any of us were going to run for office. I really did not know what to write about specifically so I asked my sponsor for help. I was encouraged to speak on who I am and the reasons I want to be elected.

I ran for the office of Avoyelles Parish 4-H Parliamentarian. The 4-H agent joked about how long the word *parliamentarian* was and how hard it was to spell. Before I presented my speech, I spelled the word correctly. After presenting my speech, I was greeted with spontaneous applause. Everyone enjoyed my remarks very much, and my opponent asked me how did I develop my speech. After everyone came back into the building after a short recess, all of us voted for the 2009-2010 Avoyelles Parish 4-H Officers. The office of parliamentarian, however, was the only office for which someone had to be elected. All of the remaining offices had only one candidate for each. I honestly did not expect to win, but when my name was announced as the winner, I was as excited as anyone could be. I was elected the parliamentarian of Avoyelles Parish 4-H. The main reason I won was the great speech I gave to the audience. It was very inspirational, and it made a difference on behalf of my victory. I learned on this day that anything can happen at any time, and that I have an obligation to remain a very ambitious, hardworking young man.

The end of the year 2009 was very peaceful; and I continued to work hard and achieve all goals for which I have set. I participated in oratory competition for a second time. However, I did not dwell on winning 1st Place, and I was the only one who expressed interest in competing. The title of my speech was *We Are the Change for A Better Future*. I emphasized the importance in hard work and education. I began to work on the speech during the night of October 30th, 2009, but I did not complete it fully until two nights later. I struggled to a high degree in developing the speech I would be most comfortable with. At the previous state convention nine months earlier, I did not enjoy myself as much. While I did have a little bit more enjoyable experience, I could not wait to return home. The convention was held on January 20th-22nd, 2010. As last time, I did not win in oratory competition this time, which made a little bitter instead of disappointed. This only triggered further my desire to just return home. Upon returning home, I felt so much better and more peaceful than ever before. Life became really well and easier for a short period of time. When I told my principal, Mr. Brent Whiddon, of the book I had written and published, he arranged for me to be recognized at a school board meeting. I was very flattered and proud to do so. From my perspective, life became so joyous and great that it could not have become any better. However, I learned that I was in for a long ride up ahead.

During the last week of January in 2010, I became great friends with a girl of whom I knew at school. She and I began to talk to each other on Facebook, we talked on the phone, and we sat with each other everyday during breakfast at school. She and I made plans to hang out at her house, and on February 7th, 2010 we did exactly that. She and her mom picked me up in the morning, and we went to McDonalds. Afterwards, we took the food and headed to her house. We watched movies, talked, and went to Pizza Hut. She and her mom drove me home later on that night. I gave her a hug and kissed her on the cheek before getting out of the car. I had such a wonderful time being with her and her mom. We made plans to hang out again during the following week. However, her mom's car broke down, which prevented me from going to her house. This is when I began to like her for more than a friend, and I became more obsessed with her than I should have. She and I could have been girlfriend and boyfriend if she was not in a relationship. This led me into an emotional downfall, which lasted into March of that year. I tried for the last two weekends in February of 2010 to hang out with her, but I was unsuccessful. There was always something beyond our control for which prevented us from seeing each other. I can remember talking to her and her friend on Facebook at 1:00 AM approximately on February 28th, 2010. He was joking with me, saying that our friend was in love with me. This made me feel extremely upset; in addition to not being able to go to her house the following morning. Afterwards, I began to pray to God about how I felt. I said to Him that I felt trapped between two walls that were closing in on me. I woke up that morning feeling as depressed and sorrowful as I ever felt before.

My emotional downfall carried over into March as it became worse. On March 16th, 2010 I went on a school field trip to see another school perform *Oliver*. We went to have lunch at Popeye's Chicken, which I did not like very much but I had no choice. I must have eaten more than I should have because I became sick two days later. The district speech rally was on the day after I became sick. Because of God, my sickness and emotional depression had absolutely no affect on my performance. I felt as if I did a spectacular job. Later on that day, I sat on the balcony of the student union and said to Jesus Christ to "help me get the tools and resources I need to put my life back on the road to long-term prosperity." I credit Him fully for not allowing my depression and sickness to affect my performance in the competition, and my emotional downfall was healed the following Monday. I learned on that following Monday that I won 1st Place in public speaking at 4-H Demonstration Day. I will never forget the smile that lit up on my face on this day for as long as I shall live. The following weekend, I gave a speech at the 4-H Junior Leadership Conference on March 27th, 2010, which inspired everyone deeply. I received more positive feedback than I could have ever imagined. Some of the others told me I could change the world and make a difference in the lives of other people. Life was seeming to become great once again. However, I would find myself in another small depression.

I began to admire a girl at the school I attend. I bought her a ten-dollar Easter basket from Wal-Mart, in addition to other gifts I purchased for her from the mall. I spent between forty and fifty dollars on her alone. It was March 31st, 2010 when I went to her house. The day did not go how I expected nor anticipated. I did not many opportunities to talk to her, and I did not enjoy myself at all. The vast majority of the time was playing video games, while I thought we were going to talk, joke, and watch movies. I did not abject to anything that happened at her house. I remember her sister's boyfriend asking me if I "had a thing for her." As reluctant as I was to tell the truth, I did so because it was entirely too much pressure for my heart to hold. I asked her two days earlier if she would date me earlier, and she said yes. When her dad learned (from me) about my feelings towards her, he did not allow his daughter and I to date because of our age difference. Fortunately, I was as disappointed as one would have expected, but I was still upset due to my feelings being crushed. Personally, I cared very little for our age difference because I believe the most important factor in a relationship is the connection shared between the man and woman. When I arrived home much later, I had begun to feel much better as I prayed to Christ for strength and stability. After this situation, I would enter the next and most dynamic phase of the journey God has set me upon: a faith and spiritual uprising.

Chapter 2

BORN AGAIN

Four days had passed since March 31st, 2010, and it was April 5th, 2010. I was sitting in the living room of my home in the afternoon watching a movie. As I looked at the door when I cousin was leaving out, I saw a lady who I had recognized strongly. It was my speech teacher from school, Mrs. KK Lemoine. I really did not expect a visit from her. As the both of us stepped onto my front porch, she informed me that she received the final scores from the district speech rally, which took place on March 19th. There was a top winner in each speech division; oral interpretation, extemporaneous speaking, and original oratory. Each top winner would be eligible to compete in the state speech rally in Baton Rouge, Louisiana. Ms. KK asked me, "Are you ready to go to Baton Rouge?!?" She informed me that I won 1st Place Superior overall, and that I am the first person from Avoyelles High School to do so. This is the greatest I have felt in a very long time prior to this day. Much later at night, I said the best prayer to Jesus Christ in my entire life. I thanked Him for giving me the strength and ability to accomplish in the midst of depression and sickness what no other person from Avoyelles High could ever do, which was win 1st Place overall at the district speech rally. This was the day that life would begin again, and it was never, ever the same again. I will cherish and honor it for as long as God lead me forward.

Beyond the day of April 5th, 2010, my love for Jesus Christ and myself began to grow immeasurably strong and inevitable. As my love for Jesus grew, I began to develop a strong sense of passion for profound greatness and a strong passion for spiritual principles such as strong character, personal integrity, and self-perseverance. I began to develop a deep love and admiration for the person who God created me to be no matter what would ever happen. I have set goals for which no person would ever attempt to set, and I developed a vision of the future that continues to the current day. Life eventually reached the point where I would cry my eyes out for Jesus

Christ, thanking Him for leading into a position where all I would ever care about was pleasing Him and achieving my goals. The first time I shed tears for Him was on June 25th, 2010 as I was on my way home from a field trip. The second time was during the evening of July 25th, 2010 when I arrived home from a walk to the store. The third time I cried for Jesus Christ was on September 6th, 2010 as I was thanking Him for ensuring the safety of my family from the dangerous neighborhood they once lived in before I was born. There would be a number of times in the future when I would shed countless tears for my Lord and Savior, Jesus Christ.

In the midst of my spiritual uprising, I remained involved greatly in the 4-H Club. By this time, 4-H had already became my favorite club. I expressed strong interest in running for State President of Louisiana 4-H. However, I needed to be a present state board member to be eligible to run. Therefore, I ran for state parliamentarian. Once every year, the Louisiana 4-H Club holds an annual event known as 4-H University. The event is always held in Baton Rouge, Louisiana on the Louisiana State University campus. It is here where the candidates for state office are elected by two-hundred delegates from the state. The trip took place from June 22nd to June 25th in 2010. When I arrived to the event, I had to get dressed in my suit, shirt, and tie immediately. There were four other individuals running against me. I was already popular somewhat because of the speech I gave at the Junior Leadership Conference a few months earlier. The delegates really enjoyed the remarks I delivered; however, I was a little frightened that I would not win. When I returned to my temporary dorm room, I called my mom and told her how I felt. Every time I told her about a situation such as this she said it really would not matter so much if I did not win. While I agreed somewhat, I always felt as if I had a duty to be victorious in absolutely everything for which I participate. I continue to feel this exact same way to the current day. When I began to stare out the window, I realized that I wanted desperately to return home. During this time, I was never a person who enjoyed leaving home for more than a day.

As for the campaign for state parliamentarian, I learned later on during the night that one of my opponents and I qualified for a runoff election, which took place the next day. For most of my second day at 4-H University, I spent much time in the LSU bookstore reading books and magazines. I fell asleep while in the bookstore as I was waiting to go to the auditorium for the runoff election. The two of us were asked to choose a sheet of paper out of a hat and answer the question that was on the paper. We also had to give another speech to the delegates. Some of the delegates told me they voted for me and that I had an excellent speech. This boosted my confidence greatly of winning. However, I became cocky and arrogant to the point where I failed to take every measure possible to be victorious. I was upset somewhat for not winning, but I was eligible to run for central regional representative since I failed to win state office. Each region had two representatives on the state executive board. Three of us ran for the two seats in the region I was from. One of the persons who ran was a previous seating representative and was reelected. I was elected as a central regional representative for the first time. This served a sort of relief from losing the race to be state parliamentarian, and it made me eligible to run for state president during the following year. I learned that Avoyelles Parish has not had a State President of Louisiana 4-H since 1979, so I felt as if I had a moral obligation to make history by not only running, but winning. I developed a burning desire to do what no man or woman from Avoyelles Parish had done in thirty-two years, which was be elected State President of Louisiana 4-H. The only thing I could think of for the next few months was accomplishing this momentous task. I told myself again and again that I would be the most excited person in the world if I would be victorious.

In addition to wanting to become state president, I ran for president of Avoyelles Parish 4-H on October 19th, 2010. I set this goal during the previous year after being elected the parish parliamentarian. As with running for state parliamentarian, I became very much cocky and arrogant about the campaign, and I failed to accomplish every measure possible to be successful. I faced two opponents; one of whom got the crowd involved heavily with his campaign techniques, while the other did not do very much. I failed within my own capacity to run the best campaign. I also forgot my book and some handouts I created. I actually reached the point where I was begging voters to vote for me, which did not help me very much. I did, however, give a really good speech for which many enjoyed. Unfortunately, I failed to become the parish president, but I pledged to return next year with a much better campaign and presentation that earn me a definite victory.

For the next few days, I was not in much of a lively, spirited mood. The best ways to describe how my heart was feeling are desolate and dry. It was mainly because I did not the win the presidency of Avoyelles Parish 4-H. The following Saturday, the day before my birthday, I was able to finally regain my sense of livelihood and strength. I was able to be reminded of the greatness for which the Lord Jesus Christ stored deep within me. I felt as if the Lord Himself was right beside me because the tears I shed for Him on that night resembled a waterfall of inevitability. My love for the Lord grew that night by one-hundred percent because the Holy Spirit re-baptized me within my heart, mind, and soul. I began to see once again the vision that Jesus instilled inside of me earlier that year. It was reaffirmed on this night that the overall strength of God in my life was as strong as ever, and I would be led into the future that He has in store. There would be some changes that would take place, but they were all part of the wonderful plan for my life.

My great desire to become the President of Louisiana 4-H would soon come to an end. As I was about to depart from a 4-H state board meeting, my ride came a little too late. This was not in my control, but it led my local 4-H agent to become upset and blame it on me, which made me very upset. In addition, transportation was sort of a problem for me as it pertained to some school-related events. I was also not very used to traveling away from home for more than a day. Prior to this incident, I was reconsidering my decision to run for state president because I did not want to be a president who could not provide the necessary leadership to get things done. With the guidance and support from God, I decided gracefully to not run for office at this time.

My next objective was to publish my second book for which I had completed in early July of 2010. The primary topic of my second book would be the importance in getting an education. I emphasized also hard work, self-sacrifice, self-determination, and strong character. It took me seven consecutive hours to complete the first chapter in the book. I procrastinated on completing the introduction and acknowledgements. After I did so, I began the publishing process, which took three and a half months to complete fully. On February 10th, 2011, *The Call of Destiny: A Liberation from Apathy, Shame, and Failure* was published. After my second book was complete, I had begun to prepare for the speech rally. Because I won 1st Place during the previous year, I felt that I had a very good chance to do so once more. This time, however, I was not sick and in the midst of an emotional downfall. I prayed time and time again to win 1st Place at the rally. After I gave my speech, I glanced at the judge's score sheet and saw that one of my scores was not as high as some of the others. I was anxious extremely to learn my final results. My speech teacher was able to find out how I did. At the end of the rally, we learned that I scored an Excellent, which is 2nd Place. I was not as disappointed as I thought I may have been, but I thanked God for giving me what I needed to do a great job. I believed always that God sees the much broader picture in every situation, even if I or others disagreed with the outcome.

All of the official speech rally results were sent to all of the schools on the following Tuesday. The date of this day was March 22, 2011. As I was talking to my principal just out of American history class, my speech teacher, who was very excited, ran to me with the results. Very much to my astonishment, we learned I actually made 1st Place Superior as I did during the previous year. I will never forget my high level of excitement that came on this day. The last time I smiled so heavily was four months earlier when I began the publishing process for my second book. On this same day, I attended an evening church service with my brother-in-Christ and best friends among many, Scotty P. Dauzat. When I attended church on this day, I thanked Jesus Christ gracefully for bestowing upon me the strength to win 1st Place at the district speech rally for a second time. As the 1st Place winner, I was eligible once again to compete at the Louisiana state speech rally, which was held on April 16th, 2011 in Baton Rouge, Louisiana on the Louisiana State University Campus. When I competed in 2010, I thought for sure I would win 1st Place. In reality I scored a 2nd Place Excellent, which was extremely wonderful because I was the first person from Avoyelles High School to ever compete at the state speech rally. Scoring 2nd Place was also very impressive for a first-time appearance. I made a solemn pledge to work as hard as I could to make history by winning 1st Place at the Louisiana state speech rally.

The bus ride there lasted for two and a half hours. After fifteen to twenty minutes from the time we left from the school, I began to cry in the name of Jesus Christ because I was reminded once again of the greatness bestowed upon me from Him. No one else saw or heard me crying, and I did not attempt to let anyone know I was. I am the type of person that no one will ever see crying as they will never find out. As I arrived on the campus, I was not nervous nor scared, and I was confident fully in my ability to give a great and spectacular performance. As I waited for my time to enter the speaking room. I practiced my speech to myself silently. When it became time to enter the room, I joined with four additional speaker who I was competing against. I was the first out the five of us to present my speech to the judge. After I did so, I asked the judge for the time that my speech lasted. I did my best to not surpass the 6-8 minute limit. However, she informed me that the length of my speech was eight minutes and sixteen seconds. I thought to myself immediately that I just wrecked my chance to win 1st Place. As I was attending to some coffee and muffins, I was informed by the coordinator that my time was not going to affect my chance of winning in a negative aspect. I was very relieved in learning of this, as it enabled me to relax my mind.

All of the competitors had to wait a few hours before finding out the final scores. As anxious I was to find out, I walked to where the scores were going to be posted five or six times approximately. The distance between my place of designation and where the scores were going to be posted was very great. The sixth time I walked to find out was when I found out my final score. I was pleased to learn for the second time I scored 2nd Place in original oratory at the Louisiana state speech rally. I was not upset or disappointed because I made a much higher score than I did in the previous year, and I still had one final opportunity to do what no person from Avoyelles High School has ever done before. Once again, I extended full praise and credit to God for bestowing upon me the tools necessary to do such a wonderful job once again.

As I looked to the future with high optimism, I began to experience a great deal of joy and laughter. During the weeks of January and much through the height of April in 2011, I was indulged with a sense of anger and "emotional dryness." The week after the state speech rally saw the beginning of an increase in peace and my ability to enjoy life. There was never a time before this as it had appeared. A few days after the rally, the Explorer's Club went on its end of the year field trip. The date of this was April 19th, 2011. We were all asked to meet in front of the school building at six o'clock in the morning, which was definitely not a problem for me since I enjoyed waking up very early. We went on a chartered bus with air-conditioning and television. Our scheduled destinations were the National World War II Museum in New Orleans, the Tiger Stadium at Louisiana State University in Baton Rouge, and the Golden Corral for lunch. The entire trip endured for seven to eight hours approximately. During the long bus ride, I primarily listened to music as I meditated on the future. I had the most joyous, pleasurable time at the places we visited, as

I was satisfied with all that we did during the trip. As we were returning home, I enjoyed heavily a harmonious time of great laughter and excitement. Many fellow club members said to me that they have never saw me laugh so much before. I personally admitted gladly that I have never had so much fun in my life prior to that day, and that it was one of the best days of my entire life. All of us continued to have a joyous time, talking and laughing and joking with one another. I never wanted this day to end, but it did sadly.

When we returned to school, we attended our school's academic ceremony in the auditorium. For the past couple of years, I was invited to the ceremony to receive several awards, including this one. This time I was rewarded with only one honor, which was recognition for being victorious at the speech rally. As always, I watched as others received numerous awards, wishing I could have received more. The only thing I do, which I did most certainly, was set a goal to receive distinguished awards such as the principal's cup, student of the year, top scholar in a particular subject area, and Mr. Avoyelles High School. I made it a fundamental obligation to meet each of these goals for which I have set, and I pledged to sacrifice to get the job done. After a few days had passed, our week-long spring vacation had begun. I spent the vast majority of this time in deep modes of prayer and meditation, and I had also written several speeches. The first speech I wrote was one I had been thinking of since the end of 2010. It emphasized American Exceptionalism and a return to the principles of hard work, individual responsibility, and personal integrity. I began writing this speech at a little after nine o'clock at night and completed it fully after three-thirty in the morning. After I did so, I laid in bed and prayed heavily to God, thanking Him for helping me complete this speech in its entirety, which I had struggled with somewhat for over a few months. The following night I wrote the second speech, which had taken over six hours to complete. It emphasized the importance in believing in yourself, making strong decisions, and strong individualism. After completing this speech, I began immediately writing an additional speech. In this speech I laid out the important principles of a strong free enterprise economy such as lower taxes, welfare reform, and education reform. While completing much of it during that early morning, I resumed it the following afternoon. I felt great that God strengthened me to complete three speeches during spring vacation. I spent the remainder of the week praying and meditating, keeping great focus on Jesus Christ.

The following Saturday I attended the annual Relay for Life Fair at the walking track just a few minutes from home. This event would last normally from ten o'clock in the morning to ten o'clock at night. I walked the track for the entire time, listening to music and visiting with friends and people I know. I always enjoyed attending outdoor events such as this because it gave me an opportunity to meet new people and enjoy the beautiful weather. After days like this, I feel a sense of great joy and am reminded if the many promises God has in store. Upon returning home later that night, my father gave me the book he has bought earlier *Reagan: A Life in Letters*.

He knew how much I admired President Ronald Reagan and his life story. After skimming through much of the book, I laid my head on my pillow and prayed to God as I fell asleep in peace and wonderful joy. The next day, May 1st, 2011, was particularly special for me because it happened to be the day that Osama bin Laden was pronounced dead. I remember this day very vividly as I was talking on the phone with my brother and read the headlines on the TV news. Tears began to approach my eyes because I recalled when my mom first showed me a picture of Osama bin Laden when I was eight years old. Before seeing that picture, I had absolutely no clue of who he was. As I had gotten older and more informed of world affairs, I began telling myself that he would never be found and that our troops should depart from Afghanistan completely. After reading the words "Osama bin Laden is dead" on the news headlines, I felt a great sense of relief and excitement. I thought of all the lives and souls that would be mended as a result of the death of Osama bin Laden. I was filled with more confidence about the possibility of lasting world peace.

From my perspective, this spring vacation was one of the best I have had in a very long time. It was marked by a reaffirmation of peace, joy, and stability. I completed three important speeches, I received a new book, and the world's deadliest assassin was put to justice. As I was really enjoying my spring vacation, it became time to return to school. The best part about returning was seeing all of my teachers and friends again. A couple of days after returning to school, one of the sponsors of our Explorer's Club called me to the front office. She asked me if I was interested in attending the LA Gear Up Conference, which is the annual meeting of all Explorer's Club officers across the entire state of Louisiana. All of the club officers in our club were seniors and were not available to attend. Since I was involved with many projects in the club, I was asked to fill in along with others. I was very reluctant to attend due to the fact that I did not like leaving home for more than a day. Also, I had planned to practice my speech on the weekend for multiple speaking engagements during the following week. As I left for school on the day of the trip, I had my bags packed and was fully prepared, but remained undecided. It was not until a few minutes before departure when I decided to attend the conference. We went on a chartered bus with air-conditioning and television. The conference took place in Baton Rouge, Louisiana and lasted for three days. We stayed at the Marriott Hotel, which was also where the conference was being held. With our school's club, it was four of us. I had much fun with all of them.

During most of the trip, I stayed with the two girls to ensure they were safe and well. The three of us talked and got along very well. One of the funniest parts of the trip was when one of the girls came to the evening dinner/event with no shoes on, and she was asked to go back to her room to put on her shoes. The entire trip was full of laughter, fun, and excitement. It also brought us closer to together as we learned more about each other. As it became time to depart back home, I was upset that the conference did not last for a longer period of time; however, I was extremely grateful for attending. I became more open to attending trips and events away from home often. It gives me wonderful opportunities to meet new and better people and learn of the much broader world for which I have yet to learn of fully. Attending this conference brought further joy and peace, and brought about a new sense of livelihood inside of me, which felt great and wonderful. I will remember this trip for many years to come.

As I returned home from the LA Gear Up Conference in Baton Rouge, I looked forward to my upcoming speaking engagements for the week. I was scheduled to speak at Lafargue Elementary School, and two days later at my own school, Avoyelles High. I realized did not need the entire weekend to prepare for these. It took me only less than half of a day to memorize the speech I had written over the spring break, which was almost nine pages. The day before my engagement at Lafargue Elementary, I read a portion of the speech to my world history class, which had only a few students. Based on their feedback, there were asking me to tone it down a little since I was speaking to elementary students. I told them I had spoken to this age group before and I have always received positive feedback. I did, however, lessened the strength of my vocabulary usage since my audience was going to consist of sixth graders. I went home and put the finishing touches on the speech for tomorrow. It was always important for me to deliver the best speeches possible. I wore a white pinstriped, navy-blue suit with a silk blue shirt and neck tie. It was always important to look the best possible when speaking, and I felt the most comfortable dressing this way on many occasions. For transportation, I made arrangements to be driven by the superintendent of schools. I was scheduled to speak at ten o'clock approximately.

As I was waiting to be picked up, I began to become really nervous as the time was getting closer and closer while the superintendent was not arriving. So I went inside and called the school board office to see if he was on his way. I learned that he had actually forgot about the engagement, but he was still available to come with me. My brother drove me to the school board office where the superintendent and I got together to go to Lafargue Elementary School. As he and I were on our way, we discussed a good deal concerning politics and issues as it pertained to the education system. The superintendent and myself got along very well, and we are good friends to the current day. When we arrived at the school, I met with the principal as she escorted the sixth grade students to the gymnasium. After they all were settled onto the floor, I was introduced as their speaker. After speaking, the kids were very impressed with my remarks as well as the fact that I had written two books at a very young age. They asked me questions regarding my story, my books, and career aspirations. I really enjoyed the time I spent with the students, and I felt as if many of them were inspired for the future.

As I returned to school for the remainder of the afternoon, I met with a lady named Ms. Carol Harris. She was associated closely with a pastor that I met a year and a half earlier. I began telling Ms. Harris of myself and the books I had written.

She told me that she would talk to her pastor in regards to me speaking at their church. I was very pleased with this, and I looked forward for this to happen in the near future. I was scheduled to speak at my school to the Jr. High students two days later. I was very popular among many of them due to the speeches I had given during the prior year at Plaucheville Elementary School. Many of them were excited that I was going to speak to them; as was I to a great extent. It was May 12th, 2011 when I spoke to them. I remember vividly as I worked to prepare everything for the auditorium, which was much fun. I was scheduled to speak at approximately fifteen minutes after one o'clock. I asked Mr. Scotty Dauzat, a teacher and great friend, introduce me, along with music. I spoke for an estimated time of thirty minutes to the students. After my remarks, a couple of students asked me questions regarding the things that inspire me as well as my plans for the future. As I was answering a student's question, the bell had rung for everyone to return to class. Everyone applauded heavily and seemed to be motivated greatly. After the students returned to class, I met with Pastor Cheryl Jackson. She was the pastor I met a year and a half earlier and the one who was associated closely with Ms. Carol Harris. Pastor Cheryl and I talked about various programs she had planned to sponsor, and told me that she was going to have me as a guest speaker.

As the day carried out, I was inspired deeply by the things for which had taken place, as I looked forward to the Cochon de Lait fair later on that evening. I returned home and changed from my professional attire into my LA Gear Up T-shirt and blue jeans. I joined with my best friend from school and his family at my favorite fast-food restaurant a few minutes from home. He and I got on one ride before attending the Anna Margaret concert, which was in junction with the fair. It was an extremely fun, exciting night with friends and amusement park rides. During the night of the fair, I was talking with a substitute teacher who was present during the speech I gave earlier that day to the Jr. High students. She informed me that many of them were out of touch with my general message; however, they loved me and were inspired by what I was doing with my life. I did not do much thinking about this until much later in my journey. The following week was the last week of school before summer vacation. I had one final speaking engagement, which was at the sixth grade graduation at Bunkie Elementary School. The graduation took place on the last day of school for everyone. I expected many of the graduates to be respectful and to listen to the message for which God laid upon my heart. However, more than many were rude, disruptive somewhat, and seemed to have been waiting for me to conclude my remarks. There were some, however, who were listening and were inspired by the message I shared. Some of them even asked to take a picture with me. After the ceremony, they served cake and drinks. I departed back to school after I enjoyed my serving.

When I arrived back to school, I ran into my friend who was waiting by the main office to learn how many days he missed during the year. As I was walking away, he said to me that if a student missed more than thirteen days, he or she would have failed for the year. So I remained by the office to find out the number of days I missed during the school year. Because I missed fourteen days, there were hours for which I needed to have excused. It was the last day of school for students, but the last day for teachers was two days later on Thursday. I was grateful in God's name to learn this when I did. If I would not have seen my friend in by the main office, I would have failed my junior year of high-school for nothing more than two days extra of absence from school. There were a few others who also went to school on the additional two days to make up for unexcused days. Most of what we did was help teachers clean and re-arrange their classrooms and help carry heavy items across the school campus. During the times we were not doing anything, I was busy on a computer trying to retrieve the video recording of the speech to the Jr. High students during the previous week. Since I had no flash drive or CD-ROM present, I attempted to email it to myself. However, the Internet system was shut down, which angered me to an extent.

Later on during the day, one of my teachers was generous enough to lend me her flash drive so I could transfer the video recording to my computer at home. She asked me to return her flash drive the next day, which I promised to do so. After entering my recorded speech to my computer at home, my next objective was to upload it on Youtube. Each time that night when I attempted to upload it on Youtube, it failed. This made me upset to the point where it led to stress. When I arrived at school for the final day, I was grouchy, upset, and stressed, primarily due to the speech not uploading on Youtube. I spent most of this day helping teachers clean their rooms and pack things away. Over in the Jr. High library, all of the books, which included an entire encyclopedia set on African-American history, were going to be thrown into the trash. The librarian, which whom I was acquainted with greatly, had given me permission to take many of the books home. I was allowed also to acquire some leftover items from Mr. Dauzat's class. As everyone was putting their finishing touches on everything, it was almost time to leave for home. I gave all of my teachers a hug, I gave my principal a firm handshake, and sat outside as I waited to be picked up. It was approaching five o'clock in the evening. As I was sitting outside and waited for my father, I looked towards Heaven and talked to Jesus Christ. I thanked Him for making me the person I am and for everything He has given me. I would always have deep conversations with God, which I enjoy to the fullest.

After my father picked me up from school, we headed to the grocery store. As I was walking in the store, I ran into some old friends from school. It came to mind to ask them about uploading videos on Youtube, He informed me that that length of the video may be too long, thus preventing it from uploading successfully. My friend informed me that I may want to consider dividing the video into two separate parts and upload one piece at a time. This is exactly what I did; and by the morning, the entire speech was uploaded on Youtube. It can be found on Youtube by typing in "Marcus Johnson speech."

As I led into the summer of 2011, I continued to seek more of Jesus Christ and gain national recognition and exposure as an author and motivational speaker. There has been so many who have promised to help me acquire exposure but they never fulfilled their promises. From my perspective, these certain individuals chose to not assist me because they see a light in me they wish they could have, but do not have it. As a believer in Christ, I realize this is only part of the journey God has placed me on. I know that my circumstances do not define who I am, but instead my ability to keep God first place and strive to the fullest. I realize also that God can take me places far bigger and better than I and all others could ever imagine. As the end of summer was approaching, I began thinking about my next book. I procrastinated somewhat in preparing to start writing it. As I did so during the previous summer, I wanted to complete the book in its entirety before school had begun. After much prayer and thinking, I was able to begin writing the book. The first chapter took me a little less than a week to complete, which I did not anticipate. I remained awake for seven to eight hours for four consecutive nights during that particular week to complete the first chapter. I completed the remaining chapters as I carried over into the next week. After completing the book, I felt very accomplished and greater as a person, and gave full appreciation to God for empowering me to write.

As I began to rest during the rest of summer until school began, I prepared for an upcoming speaking engagement. It was a back-to-school rally sponsored by my friend, Pastor Cheryl Jackson, at her church. I wrote a speech entitled "Destiny is Calling Your Success." I emphasized the importance of getting an education and having a vision for profound greatness. The event took place on August 13th, 2011, which was two days before the beginning of the new school year. I felt strongly about speaking at the program because it was a wonderful opportunity to motivate many young individuals to perform well in the upcoming school year. My great friend and mentor, Mr. Scotty Dauzat, and I went to program together. He spoke briefly at the program, saying many things that were very worth hearing. I remember Mr. Dauzat telling us that "the world tells you that you can do anything you put your mind to. That is not true; you can do anything that God puts in your heart." This statement reawakened me to the fact that there are so many forces of evil in the world seeking to influence others in a negative manner, which I will discuss in much greater detail later on in the book. After Mr. Dauzat had spoken, there were just a few more activities before it became time for me to take the floor.

As I was waiting to speak, I became great friends with Joseph Deon Jackson, Jr., the son of Pastor Cheryl Jackson. Joseph is living proof to me, as a spiritual believer, that any person can make positive choices and be someone great if he or she chooses to be. He was courteous enough to videotape my speech. After delivering my prepared remarks, I began speaking about how I became the person I am, as well as critical events that truly defined who I am. As the program was coming to a close, I met a lady from Baton Rouge, Louisiana named Catherine Adams. She was closely associated with Pastor Cheryl Jackson. Ms. Adams told me how greatly well-spoken, and how she could possibly assist me in obtaining exposure for my books and motivational speaking. We shared a very delicate conversation about certain things I could do to improve my speaking and so forth. After the program ended, I felt very strongly about my performance as well as having the opportunity to worship my Lord and Savior, Jesus Christ, which is always a great thing to do. Later on that evening, I received a call from Mr. Dauzat. He told me he was going to begin helping me gain some exposure for all that I am doing. I became so inspired by his call because it revealed to me that I do have those who are supportive on my behalf. It also showed how great of a friend and person Mr. Dauzat really is.

After the event, it became time to prepare for returning to school. It was the first day of my senior year, which I expected to feel about. I felt honestly as if it was like any other normal day of school; I was there to work hard and get an education. Most of my classes were fairly simple and enjoyable, and I made it my fundamental obligation to remain at the top of my class. I had earned myself previously a credible reputation not only as an author and public speaker, but as a positive role model. I credited Jesus Christ greatly for this because I realize that I would not be who I am without His strength and His grace. This was something I was always grateful for, and I began to make this the center of my overall message when speaking. It became important for me to share with others the work that God has done in my life and how He can make the lives of everyone else great also. I was invited to speak at youth event at a nearby church. The date of this was September 27th, 2011. Since I was given only five minutes to speak, I decided to speak directly from my heart instead of using prepared remarks. I prayed for God to put the words in my heart as well as the passion to lift them. I did not anticipate for lots of individuals to be in attendance, and I did not expect to speak so greatly without prepared remarks. Most of those who listened applauded heavily and offered wonderful compliments on my behalf. From this day forward, I would speak from my heart directly in every speaking engagement. To the current day, I have yet to use a prepared speech once again. I met with the pastor who was the keynote speaker as everything began to wrap up. I asked him if I could speak at the youth event being held at his church the following night, which he allowed me to do so gladly. This would lead to many more events throughout the month of October, which included a prayer breakfast and church congregations. All of us not only helped me grow in popularity, but gave me the opportunity to meet new people and create lasting friendships. A friendship that meant a great deal to me was that of which I made with a sheriff candidate named Damon Didier, which I will discuss more about later on.

After many of the speaking engagements had ended, I acquired more time to focus on school. As days went by, I debated whether or not I should run for president of the Avoyelles Parish 4-H Club once again. Every time I would tell myself I would not run, something inside of me would tell me otherwise. I decided eventually to run once again. In order to meet eligibility, I would have had to be a club officer at the school level. At the school level, I was the parliamentarian, which made me eligible. I ran for parish 4-H President in the previous year but was unsuccessful. However, I realized that my reasons for losing were arrogance and cockiness. These two things distracted me from doing all of the things necessary to be elected. I made it my priority to focus solely on doing what I needed to win the presidency of Avoyelles Parish 4-H, which is exactly what I did. I bought lots and lots of candy, made hangouts and posters, and did all else I could think of. I asked a friend to decorate some extra posters for which I could use to campaign. Before she could complete them for me, however, she went to New Orleans. One of my other friends who could draw very well was absent from school. My last resort was one my best friends, Heidi Lemoine-Hernandez, who is a great artist and last person I could think of. Before I could give her the sketches for the painting, she was dismissed early from school. I became a bit frustrated and discouraged somewhat due to the fact that no one was available for help. I knew, however, they did not intend to hurt me or do wrong to me in any way. For a last-minute decision, I did what I could with a few sheets if paper, which was good enough.

When I ran in 2010, I wore my school uniform and did not involve the audience in my campaign presentation. This time, however, I dressed in a suit, shirt, and tie and involved the audience to a great extent. I made perfectly sure that I did not forget anything, and I acknowledged that God was in total control of anything and everything for which may have happened. I prayed to God for the strength to do all that was necessary, and for the courage to accept what would take place. There were a couple of things that could have ruined the entire day. As I was riding the bus to school, I realized that I had forgotten my money for lunch after the election. My teacher, Mr. Joel Tassin, who I was very close with, was generous enough to lend me enough money for lunch. I repaid him the next day with the money I had forgotten at home. One additional problem was that I forgot my permission slip to attend the event. I was told by my club sponsor that I could not ride the bus with the remaining officers, which was extremely bad because I would have had no form of transportation to the youth center. This shot an instant bullet of fright up my spine. So I talked with my vice-principal concerning the issue. In following procedure, she called my mom at work and asked her if it was ok that I attend the field trip. My mom knew about the trip much long before the day of it, but I understood why she had to be called. My vice-principal said also that my mom had to have known what I was going to be doing since I was dressed in a suit, shirt, and neck tie, which made perfect sense. In thanks to God's wonderful grace, I was allowed to attend the trip, relieving the bullet of fright from up my spine.

As we arrived to the youth center, the program was previously under way. I remember seeing campaign posters on the wall of certain names of people running for parish office. While standing along the wall in tuned to the course of events, I asked two other girls running for office who the names on the posters represented.

After they told me who they were, they told me I had absolutely no worries about winning. It soon came time for all of the candidates to approach the stage to present their speeches. There were candidates for parish parliamentarian, treasurer, secretary, recreational leader, vice-president, and, of course, president. When it was time for the presidential candidates to present, I vouched to speak last because I knew that I would take much longer than the others. I knew that if I really wanted to earn the most votes, I had to set myself apart from my opponents. By wearing a suit, shirt, and tie, it gave me a greater advantage automatically. One of the girls I ran against wore blue jeans and a ripped t-shirt at the shoulder. Their speeches were short and simple, while mine emphasized a little of my life story, as well as my general vision of a better 4-H. Before I delivered my remarks, I gave each voter a pamphlet regarding my life and vision. All of the handouts were in black and white, with the exception of one color handout. I gave a giant Hershey Bar to the girl who received the color one. I had each of five volunteers hold a campaign poster as I delivered my speech, and I rewarded them with candy. After my remarks, I said to the audience, "who wants candy??". As they all screamed and yelled very loudly, I threw candy to all of them. Everyone took a twenty-minute recess and went outside after campaigning. I continued to campaign and pass out candy to voters. As we all returned inside, I could remember vividly seeing my opponent with the ripped shirt throwing out leftover pieces of my candy to some of the voters, which did not affect me in a negative manner. She did this while I was on the other side of the room assisting with training the elementary kids how to be strong, effective leaders in 4-H. This showed only what type of president she would be.

It came time for everyone to return to their seats as votes were being counted. After all of the votes were tallied completely, the results were brought to a table on stage. I caught my opponent with the ripped shirt at the shoulder on the stage looking at the results before they were announced to everyone. I could tell that really good news was in store by the look on her face. As she whispered to the other opponent, a negative look appeared on her face as well. However, I did not exceed to any conclusions until I knew for sure that I had won. All I could do at this point in time was hope that I was successful in my bid. After my name was announced as the next president of Avoyelles Parish 4-H, I became so excited that I jumped onto the stage. It was the most joyful and exciting moment in sixteen months prior to that day. I was very pleased and happy with the voters for giving me the opportunity to lead them forward. As I was about to walk out the door, there was this one voter who told me that she had voted for me. She had dark brown hair and wore glasses. This same girl said the exact same thing at the exact same spot to the person who defeated me a year earlier. This very little moment meant so much to me because the image of her saying this to my opponent in the previous year resonated in my mind. He told her thank you and smiled at her, while I did the exact same thing exactly one year after that. I remember also another little girl asking me if I was happy, and she and her friends yelled loudly to me, "bye, Marcus! Congratulations!!".

When I arrived back at school, the first place I went to was the classroom of my favorite teacher at the time, Coach Jessica Provost. She gave me the best hug that a great teacher could ever give. She was deeply proud of me for being victorious; as was everyone else who offered their hugs and congratulations. I realized that this day, October 18th, 2011 could have gone down so many roads, but God ensured that everything went exactly as planned. My prayers were answered, and I fulfilled all of the things that needed to be done, which is why I was elected the president of Avoyelles Parish 4-H for the 2011-12 school year. It was a day filled with great joy and excitement, as well as a new sense of optimism and hope for holds in the future. I felt so wonderful to have met this fundamental goal that I have set.

In addition to this were many other goals I have set such as earning the honor of receiving the principal's cup, winning first place at the state speech rally, being awarded Mr. Avoyelles High School, and becoming student-of-the-year, which was next in line of pursuit. As you can see, I have set out to accomplish many great tasks. It means absolutely everything to me to make all of my dreams a reality. I seek to bring about every desire God has stored in my heart. Whenever a person or obstacle tries to get in my way of accomplishing something I care for deeply, I take it very personally. However, it pushes me to strive much harder to be successful. This strength was tested heavily as I was seeking to be student-of-the-year. I was only an incoming freshman when I set this goal for myself to achieve. Some of the requirements included being a senior with a cumulative grade point average of 3.5 or above, which was the main criteria for eligibility. If eligibility is met, the student is required to produce and submit a portfolio with a transcript, ACT scores, self portrait, and list of extra-curricular activities. The interview with each candidate and judges was scheduled for December 14th, 2011. I knew prior to everyone else when the time was approaching to begin preparation. This was primarily because everyone else was busy with other things, while I am a multi-tasked individual. Also, because I cared about this so deeply. I prayed about it many times and envisioned myself being victorious. I stood outside on a very cold night when the sky was filled with star balls as I asked God to make me the winner.

I knew deeply in my heart that in being who I am and accomplishing all that I once have, I should be student-of-the-year. I knew also that I had everything it took to win. However, something had almost gotten in my way of succeeding. I was close to not having the required 3.5 GPA or above to be a candidate. When I learned this, I had become very upset and angry. It was all due to a minor error in my French II average. I was told I had a B average in this class, but on my report card was an F, which is what all of the French II students had. I do not believe there was a time when

I was more enraged and too anything more personal. As I was thinking in my head again and again how much I anticipated in achieving the honor of student-of-the-year, I felt worse and worse because the error was beyond my control. However, the error was corrected, and my eligibility to be a student-of-the-year candidate was no longer in jeopardy. I was soon to learn the true meaning of perseverance in my pursuit of winning. I encountered a great deal of stress, impatience, and irritation. I worked hours each day and night on completing my portfolio. I began working on it the following weekend after receiving the rubric, which was a week and a half before the due date. I was about ready to turn everything in on the following. Monday, December 5th, 2011. Before I could do so, she informed me that my extra-curricular activities were listed in the wrong format, and my phone was not in an acceptable quality. It seemed as if every time I tried turning in my portfolio there were more things to be done. While listing the extra-curricular activities in the correct format was fairly simple, the greater issue was finding a picture of myself. I tried first using a picture I had taken with the local state representative. She informed me that it was not acceptable because someone else was in the picture with me. I attempted to use one I had taken with a city councilwoman, but she told me it was too small. I believed, personally, that all of this was very petty and that none of it should have been of issue.

I spent the entire day in pursuit of getting a photo for the portfolio. I was told I could receive an old school photo from the publications teacher. A publication student promised to help me acquire one. He never showed up in the library, where I paced with great, unspeakable frustration and impatience. It was not until an hour and a half later when he showed up to the library with the publications flash drive. It would not load completely on the librarian's computer, so he and I went to the publications classroom to get the photo. After I received the photo, I was able to resume working on and perfecting my overall portfolio. I worked on it all the way until the hour it was due. As a perfectionist, I ensured everything was correct and the way it was supposed to be, which it was. After I turned everything in, the only thing that was left to complete the interview before a panel of judges. Due to state law, there had to be two African-American judges and two Caucasian ones. This is to ensure fairness without biased discrimination, which I am in total favor of.

In the interview, they asked questions regarding my life story, career aspirations, and school activities. After the interview was complete, I greeted each of the judges with a handshake out of kindness and respect. All that was left to do was keep one-hundred percent trust in Jesus Christ. I felt very strongly about my portfolio, interview, and as s student in all that I had accomplished. I desired so greatly to be student-of-the-year at Avoyelles High School, and I was overwhelmed with anxiety. One of the persons I was competing against was the top student in the class of 2012. He had a 4.0 GPA and very high test scores, in contrast to my 3.8 GPA and average test scores. I felt just a little intimidated by this in regards to the competition. I began immediately to grow out of this insecurity by keep faith in my Life, Lord, and Savior,

Jesus Christ. I re-evaluated the person He created me to be. We learned the results about a week after the interview. As anxious and impatient as I had become, I was attempting to find out before everyone else. I do this with everything I participate in; primarily because I strive always for the best and never less. Never before had I been overwhelmed with so much anxiety, and it persisted for about a week. It was not until the day I learned who won when all of the anxiety had disappeared. I learned who won before everyone else did.

I was sitting in the library completing work for French II as a student office worker came in to get the results for them to be announced on the intercom. As I was working, I saw the librarian showing her the results. When the student worker saw the results, she said the name aloud, without notice of me being able to hear. After I realized I did not achieve the honor of student-of-the-year, a profound sense of stillness approached inside of me. As strongly and passionately as I wanted to win, I was not disappointed nor hurt because I asked God previously to strengthen me to deal with anything for which may have taken place. However, I did wish that I was victorious in achieving the honor of student-of-the-year. I remember walking around the library as I coped with the stillness in my heart. The librarian could tell I was not very happy with the outcome, so she tried her best to talk some hope into me. While I was not disappointed, negative thoughts began to plague my mind. The main thought was all of my hard work and accomplishments as a student did not account for anything to those at Avoyelles High School. I also felt a sense of vulnerability from not winning. So I asked Mr. Brent Whiddon, my principal, for his thoughts on me as a person and student. He said to me that I was a great student and that his job would be much easier if more students at Avoyelles High were more like me. While this did encourage me somewhat, God pulled me back into shape immediately as the day carried out. Instead of resorting to bitterness and cynicism, I would maintain faith in Jesus Christ for the future. I knew always that He is in total control of everything that would happen in my life. In remembering who God created me to be, I realized I had absolutely nothing to worry about, even if I chose to do anyway. It was time to shake the loss off completely, and strengthen the vision of greatness God has stored in my heart. As long as I know what my future holds in store, I would always be filled with great joy and peace, as well as the motivation to advance as far as my dreams would take me.

It was not until of a couple of years ago prior to this time when I realized the true potential within myself. After this happened, I began to believe in and admire myself for who I am. More importantly, many of the negative things about me departed as greater things came in. As this was happening, I would become a stronger, wiser person over time. Many people began to notice this change about me for which was occurring. When some people got to know who I was, they reacted with hostility and animosity. Some would say negative, offensive remarks, and regard me as something I am not. This stemmed most likely from jealousy, envy, and even racism, possibly. Along with a great deal of lecturing from teachers, all of this led me into a deep-seated anger and bitterness that carried over into the new year, 2012. I believe it was stemmed mostly from a sense of pride in who I am. Something such as this had taken place during the beginning of 2011. It reached the point the point where I was saying to myself I wanted to "cut these people's throats out with a knife." I even envisioned myself doing so, which was not a good thing to do. This time in 2012, however, the anger I felt was very much stronger and lasted much longer. I resorted to name-calling, bigotry, and cynicism for what some others could become. The anger would soon become bitterness, and I actually had visions of hurting some people, physically and verbally. All of this led me to dislike heavily the school that always held a special place in my heart. I considered being a homebound student, and told myself if things ever became "too bad," it would be time to "get out of dodge."

There were several specific events that either worsened or brought out the bitterness I was carrying around. One certain situation was an argument that occurred between a good friend and myself. While she and I always shared a great friendship, we had our differences at times; and the argument we had certainly showed it. It was in the morning time during breakfast at school. I had just been served my food in line and was about to find a seat. As I was walking by, someone I knew asked me to sit next to him. I failed to realize how much of a grave mistake I was about to make. The seat I sat in was the exact same seat that my friend would reserve for herself every morning. Before I sat down, the guy in the next seat put her book bag onto the floor. As she was walking to her seat, she accused me of moving her belongings, which was not true. In addition to this incident, I was very uncomfortable with how she regarded this particular seat as her owns and made others who sat in this seat to move. I said to myself I would deal with her heavily if she would attempt to cause any trouble. When she came over and accused me of moving her stuff and tried to make me move, I began immediately shouting and swearing at her at her as she did somewhat also. We caught the attention of others in the cafeteria. After a few minutes, the both of us began to settle down and stop fighting. This would be the only fight my friend and I would have, as we generally got along greatly. Later on during the day, we apologized to one another in regards to the fight we had and remained the best of friends.

The next incident could probably be considered more petty than normal, but it was larger in worth. It was in speech class as we began our debate unit. Each person met with his or her partner to decide what team they would debate. Once this was done, we decided what topic and between negative and affirmative. My team was going to debate the issue of abortion with our opposition team. However, my partner and the opposition team had chosen that my team would argue in favor of abortion, which is not something I was going to do. As a devout Christian and person of strong faith, I was not about to argue in favor of something of this magnitude under any circumstances. The thing which angered me the most, however, was that they made the decision without asking for my opinion first. So when the teacher returned to the class, I told her exactly what happened. We all discussed it and agreed that my team would not argue in favor of abortion. It was not so much their decision for which angered me, but the fact they did not ask me about the decision. This gave me the idea that I was not important to them. I was in this speech class for three years to this time, in contrast to their first year. The two people who were responsible for the establishment of the speech/drama department at Avoyelles High School during my freshman year were myself and an individual who was in a higher grade than me at the time. I was a sophomore taking the class with juniors and seniors who were expected to have much more experience than me, but I outperformed each and every one of them in the class and at the speech rally. So I took it very personal when they banded together and made that decision without me. While I did get my way in the end, I was still upset at the entire situation; and it made my bitterness only much worse than it was.

As I stated earlier, the anger-turned-bitterness that I had derived from the way I was regarded by some for who I am. It stemmed also from the fact that they looked down upon the greater things in life, and envied those who seemed to have more than them. Due to the fact they saw I had such a strong relationship with Christ, I valued character and hard work, and I was not living up to their hopeless standards, they resented me for it. In smaller ways, they hated my guts because I was very much different. It even reached the point where I felt strongly as if some of them were out to get me. It really seemed to be true during one of our club days at school. In our Fellowship of Christian Students Club meeting, I got up and spoke to everyone about the day when Jesus changed my life forever. The club sponsor was not present during the meeting. There was much noise taking place as I was speaking, which aggravated me to a great degree. I said to them in a firm voice to quiet down as I was talking. I said also that it was many of them who were making terrible decisions and that they needed to seek God in their lives. A couple of hours later was the SADD Club meeting, where I was club president. I spoke to the members about the powerpoint presentation we had planned to do for the Jr. High students. I started speaking also about exemplifying the behavior that our club stands for so we could be strong role models for the rest of those in the school. I said also for us to not be making the very decisions that our club's platform stands against. I expected for them to be enlightened and to agree since we were all members of Students Against Destructive Decisions. On this day, however, Students Against Destructive Decisions became Students *For* Destructive Decisions. I found it really amazing, but not surprising, when the club began to defend wild parties, alcoholism, drugs, etc. One of the members even said I "should not turn it down before I try it." As astonished as I had become, I was ten times as mad and frustrated. Besides the fact they defended what is deliberately wrong, they did so as members of a club for which is supposed to fight against the very things they were defending. This is the exact same thing as being a parent to a child and treating him or her with hate, abuse, and neglect, which is the opposite of love, guidance, and respect. I did not know what to believe beyond this period. Not only did my bitterness become much worse, but Avoyelles High School no longer had a club to speak out against the things that are destroying the lives of young and older people alike.

The next morning as I was standing outside with friends before the beginning of our first period class, a friend told me "there's a (bleep) load of kids wanting to kick your (bleep)." She was referring to the kids who were present during the Fellowship of Christian Students Club meeting. My friend overheard them say this yesterday about the meeting. The first thought that came to mind was Jesus Christ. He was mocked, laughed at, criticized, beaten, and crucified for all of the things He sought to bestow into the minds, hearts, and souls of everyone in the world. Jesus said to the world that all of His followers would be persecuted for His name's sake, which was exactly what was happening to me at the time. Upon hearing my friend tell me the news, I was not afraid, upset, nor discouraged. This did not even contribute to my bitterness because I remembered what Jesus said about situations like this. Usually I would report something of this manner to the principal, but in this particular situation I did not. I knew God was in total control and would protect me from any possible harm and evil. He would also strengthen me to deal with every obstacle that threatened me in any way, shape, or form.

As days and weeks had gone by, no one said or attempted to do anything to me in a negative manner, which was absolutely no surprise to me at all. It was so amazing how they stood so tough while I was not around, but demonstrated a profound sense of weakness by not standing up to me. All of this was leading me continuously to the point of disliking school like I never have before. A couple of weeks later, I was walking through the hallway and was approached by a fellow SADD Club member. She told me the club needed to meet with me later on that following afternoon. She did not give any specific reasons for why. After she told me it was important, I asked her if I would somehow be president no longer after the meeting, and she said she did not know. As I made it to gym class, I became so enraged and worked up it was beyond control. It reached the point where I actually felt as if I wanted to really hurt someone, physically. I felt grateful that I was in gym class in contrast to English or biology, which would have been terrible. The fact I may be stripped as club president for no legitimate reason is what angered so. I went to ask out club sponsor what the meeting would be about. She told me that she knew nothing of the meeting, which revealed to me that some of the club members may have been planning something in secret. I was determined to halt any and all schemes these guys may have had in mind. So I went to my mentor to tell him the situation that was taking place. He and I went into the main office and called for the club member who told me about the meeting. According to her, they wanted to meet with me to discuss the powerpoint presentation we were planning to present to the Jr. High students. While feeling a sense of relief, I felt deep within as if some of the club members had a plot in mind to kick me out of office; but I thanked God for assisting me in solving this properly and ensuring that nothing went wrong. Beyond this issue, I would encounter additional conflicts with certain people, which all derived from jealousy, ignorance, and hate. All of the things that were happening; conflicts due to jealousy, feelings of not be recognized, and, most of all, my increasing anger and bitterness would lead me eventually to a breaking point: sickness.

The final day of my deep-seated, profound sense of anger would approach, which I did not anticipate. The date was January 17th, 2012. I remember telling my teacher, Ms. KK, how I was feeling. Out of all she said to me, the one thing I remember her saying most vividly is that I am different from everyone else and very unique. I also remember seeing her smile at me as I walked away. The rest of the day carried on as I took it easy and fought through as best as I could. It was not until much later on that night after I was home from school when I told my mom I wanted to stay home the following day. She also thought that a break would be beneficial for me. My mom is a very understanding person who cared always for what I may have been experiencing. I also began to develop cold symptoms. As a couple of days had gone by, my throat became sore, my body became weak and very achy, and I caught a growing fever. By the end of the week, everything became much worse. I called Ms. KK at school to tell her the reason I have been absent from school for so long. I had become so sick that I had no desire for food, and if I attempted to eat anything, I was not able to complete the meal. I had no hormonal reactions, which had not taken place in a long time prior to becoming ill at this time. The only things there were most relevant in life at this point were empty cleanix boxes, my bed, and much sleep.

When I became a little better during the following week, I was able to attend school for senior picture day. When I arrived at school, however, I became weak once more. I went to the nurse station, and they called home. I was picked up and brought home immediately after I had taken my pictures. Later on that day, my parents took me to the emergency room. We thought it may have been asthma, but I was diagnosed instead with bronchitis. As hard as it was to talk, I asked the doctor if the bronchitis could be healed, and he told me it could be. He prescribed me multiple medications for treatment, and told us to come back to the emergency room if the prescribed medications did not work properly. The prescribed medications were helping very well, which was great on my behalf. As with the medications, a great deal of rest was needed so I could recover fully. I was out of school for a week and a half, which was the longest I had ever been absent from school in a very long time prior to this time period. This gave me much needed time to overcome the things I was experiencing before.

By the end of the week, I was much better to the point where I could walk around and eat food again. I spent the weekend the following the weekend with my sister-in-law at my brother's house while he was on vacation. Upon returning home, much of the bronchitis had been healed. However, I developed this desire to grow again. I realized it was my illness that led away my deep-seated bitterness and anger. After this, I desired for things to return to the way there were prior to my anger period. I sat in my room and prayed for God to lead me forward and help me learn more of history and philosophy. I realized this illness had done more good than bad. It had not only washed away the overwhelming anger I held, but it provided me an opportunity to grow stronger and strengthen my relationship with Jesus Christ. The entire experience made me realize fully how great I am as a person, and inspired me to strive more diligently to achieve the goals I have set. There are many who have been tempted to give up on achieving the things God put in their hearts. Because I have such an indomitable, unwavering faith in the Creator of the Universe, I know how to deal with certain situations such as the one I have just overcome. I am also able to remain greatly positive and allow Him to continue to lead me into the future He has in store.

It was not until I returned to school when I realized how much I missed it. There were some who were very pleased to see me again, while others remained indifferent. Ms. KK was very excited to see me again at school. A friend of mine said to me that she thought I may have died. The best part about the entire situation was having no longer any feelings of anger and bitterness as well as no visions of fighting with or hurting any person or persons. It was a time to reinvigorate God's strength within me, and continue to fulfill my important obligations, which is exactly what happened. I also began to excel and become much better known throughout Avoyelles Parish, Louisiana. I was the keynote speaker at approximately six different programs for African-American history month, which generated myself a great deal of name recognition. On February 16th, 2012, I was the keynote speaker for the second time at a parental involvement fair, which was a school-related event. I reached the point where people from all throughout town knew who I am. I would walk into a store and individuals of whom I have never met would speak to me and shake my head. I could be walking on the sidewalk sometimes and people driving on the street would either wave at or shout to me. As many times before, people would tell me I have the potential to become the nation's president in the future. Ever since I have been told this beginning at the age of 15, I have learned much more about life and what it is about. I have also become far more aware of the fundamental challenges of our time and have addressed them on numerous occasions.

As I led into the month of March, it was time to once again prepare for the district speech rally. This was the fourth consecutive year I competed in the competition. Every year at the rally, there are four different categories to sign up for. There were original oratory, extemporaneous speaking, interpretative reading, and drama/theater. Usually I would compete in just original oratory. This year, however, I competed in both original oratory and extemporaneous speaking. I, along with the remaining speech/drama class, competed in drama competition. We presented a portion of the play *Much Ado About Murder* that we presented earlier in the year at school. For the oratory competition, I presented a speech on ridding abortion from the Earth, which I had written in October of 2011. I had planned originally to present a different speech that I wrote on education. After presenting the abortion speech for an assignment, Ms. KK and I decided to go with this one. I felt stronger about the abortion speech because I was deeply passionate for this issue, and the competition was held always at Louisiana College, which is a private, Baptist school. The speech on abortion as written originally was much longer in length than it needed to be. Ms. KK and I worked with the speech up to the day of the rally. As for the extemporaneous competition, I did not have to work on anything until arrival at the college.

All of those competing had to enter a room and pick a random piece of paper with a written topic out of a glass bottle. Upon doing so, each of us were allowed thirty minutes to complete a speech and research information on the Internet if needed to do so. The topic I received was the following: "should the United States pursue a more active role in world affairs?". I was hoping previously to receive a topic such as this one. Because I was very knowledgeable in this subject area, there was absolutely no need for me to research anything on the Internet. I was also able to complete my speech within ten to fifteen minutes of the total half hour that was provided. After completing my extemporaneous speech on paper, it was time for me to deliver my speech for oratory competition. I felt more hopeful for and had greater confidence in my performance this year in contrast to the previous year, and I did not ask the judges any questions as I did during the previous year. I had great faith in the Lord God Jesus Christ that I did very well, and knew that my prayers would be answered as they always have been. As for the extemporaneous competition, I felt very strongly about my performance.

After we ate lunch in the student union, it was time for us to present our play for the drama competition. The only audience members present were the judges for the competition. We were greeted with spontaneous applause and wonderful compliments. I, along with another actor in our group, were told we had the perfect look for being a famous actor. I was told by one of the judges that I look like Denzel Washington, which was one of the best compliments I had ever received. In addition to the speech rally, there was a campaign rally being held by then-presidential candidate Ron Paul in the next building to us at Louisiana College. I wanted greatly to attend but could not due to the drama competition. After we presented our play, I wanted to run over and see him but it was time for the speech class to depart back to the school. It was not until the following week when we received the results from the judges. We did not receive the official results until the following week after that. According to the email Ms. KK received, I won first place in both original oratory and extemporaneous speaking, which qualified me to compete at the state speech rally. While I was very glad with the results, I was too focused on preparing for state competition than becoming too comfortable. I was competing at state rally once again, but for the final time.

I had one final opportunity to win first place at the state speech rally. This year, however, I was competing in two competitions; original oratory and extemporaneous speaking, along with the play for drama competition. I prayed with all of my heart to Jesus Christ for all that I needed to perform the best. I asked Him to ensure that I do what no other person at Avoyelles High School has ever done before, which is win first place at state rally. This was the third time I competed at the state level in the speech rally. The two previous times I have gone, I anticipated victory but did not achieve it. I improved greatly in my speaking ability over time, and achieved a higher score each time I competed. Due to other things in my life that were happening, I had little time to think about the upcoming state rally. I knew deep within my heart, however, that this was my year. I knew within myself that everything would go exactly the way it should. There was no need for practice because I had already became an expert at public speaking, and I knew that Jesus Christ Himself would put in my heart what to speak with the passion to follow. I did, however, deliver my abortion speech for original oratory to Ms. KK numerous times for critiquing. As for the extemporaneous speaking, there was no need for any practice because I would not learn what my topic would be until I arrived to the university. I chose to not research anything on the Internet because I felt as if I had known much already about current affairs.

As I was riding on the school bus to Louisiana State University in Baton Rouge, all I chose to focus on was my Lord and Savior, Jesus Christ. I realized this would be my final opportunity of a lifetime to win first place at the state speech rally, and I had the ultimate faith in Him that it would happen for sure. I remember when my very good friend, Mr. Frank Akridge, encouraged me to close my eyes and envision myself as the winner. This is exactly what I did as I prayed before I began speaking. For the oratory competition, I gave a fairly good performance in my opinion. It was in the extemporaneous speech where I did my absolute best. My topic was whether or not should high-school graduates be required to pass a drug test for eligibility to receive taxpayer-funded assistance for college. I was in favor strongly of it, and spoke primarily of it from my heart. I felt very strongly about my performance. The judge told me later on that I did the best job, which was long before the official results were finalized. After the speech competitions were complete, it was time for us to compete in the drama competition. Some of the kids in my group had chosen to leave early to prepare for prom, which was later on that evening. In my opinion, this was a very petty and illegitimate reason for leaving early. Because they left early, we did not learn that day the results of the competitions, and they were not able to heart their critique from our performance. It was only Ms. KK and myself who received our critique from the judges. I was complimented very greatly on my performance in the play, and was greeted heavily for not leaving early as the others did. Even though I went to prom also, I chose to not leave from the university early so that I could learn how I could improve my acting ability.

After this, it was time to depart for home. It was not until a few days later when I learned that I placed a Superior in extemporaneous speaking at the state speech rally, which is 1st Place! I learned the results from the university's website. Ms. KK learned the results previously and wanted to surprise me at the academic awards ceremony, which was held during the following week on May 1st, 2012. I felt a little upset that I ruined the surprise; however, I was as proud as ever for doing what no person from Avoyelles High School had ever done before, which is win 1st Place Superior at the state speech rally. I realized I competed against many of the best speakers throughout the entire state of Louisiana, and defeated each and every one of them. I credited Jesus Christ fully for coming through on my behalf, and was reminded furthermore of the true strength of Him inside of me. At the awards ceremony on May 1st, I was awarded with a medal for winning at the state speech rally, as well as the Principal's Cup, which I was flattered highly in receiving. I arrived to the ceremony thirty minutes late approximately, but it was exactly as Ms. KK was calling me to the stage to receive the speech award. Everyone assumed I had planned to do that originally, which was very fond in thinking about. In contrast to the three previous academic ceremonies, this was the best one I have attended ever.

A couple of weeks later, I had done some motivational speaking at some other schools. I also spoke to the Jr. High students at my school, which went very well. All of them were very inspired and uplifted by my words. I spoke to them on May 16th, 2012, which was exactly four years after the day I graduated from Jr. High myself. This would be the very last speech I would present at Avoyelles High School as a student. From all that was happening, it was more than clear that God was doing profound work in my life. I was always deeply grateful for this, and I continued to strive for more of His greatness. This was the most important thing in the world to me. All things that would serve as a great threat to this would be dealt with heavily until the end. I promised God I would never be perfect, yet I would uphold my commitment to Him as I strive to achieve the things He stored in my heart at birth. In an effort to become a stronger person in His eyes, I had to not only accept, but to endure the challenges He would align in my journey. The most difficult situations I have dealt with in the past involved feelings for certain girls and relationships. From my perspective, they are the most difficult of any issues a person would ever have to go through. The main reason for this is that pursuing a successful relationship with someone involves a great deal of work. If the situation consists of any other, the relationship cannot and will not be beneficial in the long-term.

During early 2012, I had become great friends with my best friend's then-girlfriend's sister. She is a very strong Christian, really nice and considerate, and has a pure heart. We got along very well, and became closer and closer as the weeks went by. However, our friendship was over Facebook, which was of no concern to either of us. There came a point where she began to admire me for more than a friend, which flattered me. I believed as if I had feelings for her also. Much to our dismay, her father would not allow her to date any guys who did not share the same skin color. I read this in a message immediately after waking up from a long sleep. This did not bring any personal shame to me for my skin color, and it did not tempt me by any measure to think less of who I am as an individual. It still did not reverse the admiration and feelings I shared for her. I was so upset that I did not attend school the next day. I continued to feel sort of down about it for the two weeks following. A reliever somewhat was being able to hang out with her on a day during spring vacation. She, her sister, my best friend, and myself hung out together. We ate at McDonalds, shopped at Wal-Mart, saw a movie, and went to their home. After we all spent time together, my best friend and I had ordered pizza, picked up his grandmother and a friend, and went to his house to watch a movie I bought. All of this took my mind off of the entire situation, but I still struggled to a certain extent. I prayed to move forward in peace and stability.

During the next week, I began to feel very much better. The following day I became better fully after being honored for student-of-the-month at the school board office. It felt so wonderful to be peaceful at heart once more, but it lasted only a few short days. I had no earthly idea that I was about to enter into the most dramatic experience of my entire lifetime so far. Far greater than anything I have ever experienced, it would truly define every aspect of who I am as a person.

Chapter 3

Dramatic Experience

Following the evening after being honored as student-of-the-month, I would become acquainted greatly with the friend that my best friend and I picked up while hanging out. Our friendship began when we were at my best friend's house a week earlier. We became friends on Facebook and began to communicate with one another. It had taken only a day for she and I to begin admiring one another beyond friendship. We began to talk on the phone and flirt heavily. It was not until the following weekend when our relationship began to return instability into my life once again. She and another good friend of mine at the time were talking on the phone while I was present. The words she was saying and text messaging to him was making me feel extremely uncomfortable. My then-friend told me he was going to talk to her more and see what type of person she really is. A few hours later, I received a text message from him telling me how much she loved and cared about me. However, I developed a slight fear that she would grow feelings for him and abandon me, which stemmed from the fact that she was flirting with fourteen different guys at the exact same time. I became better somewhat within the next few days. As I was sitting near the football field at school reading my Bible, a teacher who I was very good friends with came over by me and we began to talk. I told her what was bothering me, and she said to me many things that continue to resonate with me to the current day. She told me to not focus on relationships, and to get the best education. She encouraged me to believe in myself, which I did, and to find myself so that I could know truly what I desire out of a lady emotionally, mentally, and spiritually.

It was the following Sunday, April 22nd, 2012 when my then-girlfriend began to show her true side, which was an extremely terrible day for the both of us. She and I had planned to see a movie together, but she cancelled without reason. She also began to become very upset with me for absolutely no reason. I became so upset and very hurt emotionally on this day. I was walking around outside feeling very bad, and I even felt as if my time on Earth was finished. These feelings were not of a suicidal nature, but instead consisted of being too Godly and kind to live in this type of world. I did not begin to think less of who I am, but because of who I am that I had no use for others. I realized immediately that none of this was true, and the only reason I felt this was being treated like a criminal for no reason by my girlfriend. I felt so terrible I had to call my good friend, Scotty P. Dauzat, to pick me up and take me some place. Just after I called him, my then-girlfriend began to apologize for all that she did, which I accepted. She then told me that her grandfather was very sick and about to die. After fifteen to thirty minutes approximately, she sent me a text message saying that he passed away. My heart shot through my chest and through the asphalt literally.

When Mr. Dauzat and I arrived at a local Shell, my then-girlfriend called me as was crying very terribly. I did my absolute best to console her. Her grandfather's death hurt me also on the inside. After a while my cellular phone began to run out of battery strength, as Mr. Dauzat and I arrived at a cross at a nearby cemetery. He and I would come here often to pray and fellowship as brothers-in-Christ. We discussed relationships, sex, and marriage. As a brother-in-Christ, Mr. Dauzat would encourage me in these areas spiritually, and to follow God's purpose. After our discussion, I returned home, prayed, and took very short walk at the track close to where I lived. As for the next couple of days the relationship between my then-girlfriend and I began to improve much. I comforted her for the loss of her grandfather, and even brought my cellular phone to school so I could communicate with her. We hardly ever got the chance to spend time with one another in person. So we began to meet in town on some days after school. A couple of times I was forced to receive rides from others outside of my family. It did not matter to me because I loved and cared for her very much at the time. We would begin to send each other text messages from the we had awakened in the morning to very late at night. It seemed as if our relationship was going very well and smoothly. However, she began to become very inconsiderate and evil. She would get angry over small, childish things, which brought me through emotional pain and bondage. During the first day of my high-school graduation week, she and I met at the library in town. She was very unaffectionate and irritable, which made me less attracted to her. So I stopped talking to her for a few days.

During graduation practice at school the next day, I learned that a girl who I had been admiring since November of 2011 just broke up with her boyfriend. She had been admiring me too, and she said earlier on that she would date me if she was single. So I asked her to be my girlfriend, and she said yes. I gave her a hug and asked if we could spend much together during the Summer, which she responded positively. We talked on the phone later that day as we got to know each other a little bit better. As for the other girl I was with, it was over for that point in time. My new girlfriend was very considerate, kind, sweet, and very beautiful. She even attended my senior graduation, which after I received from her my very first kiss. I really loved her with all of my heart, as she loved me the same. She came to my house two days after my senior graduation. The date of this was May 26th, 2012. We kissed, hugged, touched, and laid next to each other. This was the first time I have ever had a girl in this type of capacity. She wanted to have sexual intercourse, but we did not because I made a solemn oath to God previously that I would wait until I am married to do so. She and I continued to do all of the things we were doing and enjoy our time together. The only negative aspect of the entire day was that she sneaked out of her home before her mom was aware that she was gone. She also lied about where she went to when her mom sent her a text message. While she and I were in the bedroom, I would become paranoid when I heard footsteps because I thought her mom called my house phone. I became even more afraid when her mom actually found out she left. I thought she was going to call the police on her and have them trace her phone to find her location. So it came across my mind for us to leave the house and go someplace else. I was so paranoid and afraid that I could not even realize that was the worst thing ever to do.

I was so scared and worried I could not think clearly. My girlfriend was able finally to convince her mom that everything was alright. After a few hours had gone by, her mom became more worried and wanted her home. It had taken me about forty-five minutes to walk her home, which was a six-mile walk from my house. During my six-mile walk back home, I could not stop looking back towards her home. As I was walking on the dirt road, I was nearly bitten to death by a poisonous snake. A man driving his car behind me killed the snake by running it over with his car. He drove up to my left side and encouraged me to be careful and cautious when walking on that particular dirt road. Approximately twenty to thirty minutes later, I was nearly one foot away from being rundown by a massive truck. If I did not have God's grace upon me on this day, I would have either been seriously injured or killed. Upon arriving home, I sent a text message to her mom's phone, asking her if she made it home safely. It was not until the next morning when I found out she was punished for sneaking out. She was not able to talk on the phone or send text messages, and she was not as active as I was on Facebook. This meant there was no possible way of she and I communicating, and her mom did not tell me when she was going to be off of punishment.

I slipped into the most extreme depression of my entire life at this point. The main thought that plagued my mind was the thought of my girlfriend's mom possibly making us end our relationship due to what happened. It plagued my mind for the next couple of days. Because I became so depressed, I began to feel as if I was losing myself. All of the wonderful work God had done in my life over the years was in great jeopardy. Each time I attempted to focus in getting into college and reaching God's destiny, I would be interrupted by the thoughts of my relationship. She was released from her punishment after a few days, which made me feel better. However, she would become punished again and again for other things at home, which prohibited from communicating with one another. Eventually our relationship would end as a result. I had absolutely no clue that the day she came to my house would be the very last time I would ever see her. While she and I were just twenty feet from her house,

I held her in my arms heavily. The last words we ever said to each other were "I love you." I still think about her sometimes to the current day, and have thoughts of being with her once more. As months had gone by, I would have multiple dreams about her, and even needed to talk to a pastor about the situation. The talks with the pastor assisted somewhat for the better, but she still would not leave my mind fully.

As the summer of 2012 progressed, all that would plague my mind were relationships issues. I reunited with my previous girlfriend from the early spring, but it became as terrible as it could ever be. All she did was taunt my emotions to the fullest extent and take advantage of me. We would break up, get back together, break up, and get back together again. It became nothing more than a vicious cycle, which was very unhealthy for me. I reached the point where I became more unstable than at any other time in my life. I would stand around outside feeling beyond terrible. I laid in bed all the time, feeling lifeless and depressed. It was all over a person who was selfish, extremely mean, and cared nothing for me. My mind was plagued to the point where I was not able to begin college in the Fall semester. If I would have began in the Fall semester, I would have most likely not been able to finish to the end. The worst of the entire situation was that I felt as if my strong, committed relationship with Jesus Christ was reaching a compromise, and this furthered my mind into a much worse state.

Through all that was happening to me, I continued to pray to Christ and hold to Him as strong as I could. I had a conversation with a minister friend of mine in regards to my relationship issues, feelings for my previous girlfriend, and my faith in Jesus Christ. She referred me to places in Holy Scripture that emphasized relationships, sex, and the importance of morality. She also encouraged me to save all for which God has given me for my wife in the future, which made perfect sense to me. At this point, I knew how important it was to rid my girlfriend at the time from my life forever. While I wanted greatly to do so, the courage had not approached my heart just yet. Every person I could think of encouraged me strongly to end all ties with her, but I continued to justify her reasoning for being who she is. The fate of our relationship approached finally, which ended primarily in a brief, verbal fight.

My cellular phone was turned off for lack of bill payment. I downloaded a free text messaging app so I could communicate with others, and I continued to talk to her. The purpose of our fight was the fact she would break up with me and get with me again consistently, which angered me. The final conversation between she and I as girlfriend and boyfriend took place on the night of July 6th, 2012. She was implying to me that she wanted only to be friends, and that she was not sure if she really loved me or not. I became very angry about this because it continued to take place. I became very fed up with being mistreated for illegitimate purposes, and I revealed my frustration to her. I felt much better after doing so, but I became tempted heavily again and again to call her and talk to her again. As the days and weeks were advancing, much deep-seated anger for her began to develop. I began referring to her with insulting names, and desired to let her know how I felt. I was also feeling extremely vulnerable and depressed from all that has happened. There were even days when I became tempted to call my old girlfriend and see about getting with her again, but I knew I could not do that. It was not stemmed from desperation, but from the unfulfilled love I had for her.

My mind was plagued, and every time I would feel hopeful somewhat, I would lose it immediately. I felt uncertain as never before about the future, and I had no longer the ability to focus on the things that make my life great and worth living. As time went on, glimmers of hope began to develop. I knew that the only way forward was reaching out to Jesus Christ through consistent prayer and meditation. I needed to remind constantly that Jesus never gives us more than we can bear. The only way out of this crisis was through Him and absolutely no other way. Many of His greatest miracles are fulfilled through people, and this is exactly what Christ did to rescue me from this terrible downfall. After a luncheon with my minister friend, she and I had driven to her husband's auntie's house. I told her I had written several books and am a motivational speaker. She was very impressed and complimented me heavily. She had also written down my phone number and told me she would give it to her brother, Marshall Pierite, whom would assist me in obtaining exposure for what I do. A week later, he and I went for a drive and had a long, deep conversation about God and principles of faith. We stopped by his office for a minutes also. He said he would give to President Obama a copy of my books, which is still in progress to the current day. He travels to Washington, D.C. often, and he had given the books to the President's senior advisor, Ms. Valerie Jarrett. The President still has yet to receive the books and get in contact with me. Mr. Pierite also took me with him and his family to South Dakota to speak a Christian youth rally.

It was the trip to South Dakota for which God used to rescue me and make me strong once again. As the night before the trip had approached, I became reluctant of it and nearly reconsidered about attending. However, I felt strongly as if I knew something great would happen during the trip. I attended as planned originally, but I had only less than a couple of hours of sleep due to a Monster energy drink from earlier in the day. On the trip were Marshall Pierite, his wife, his daughter and her friend, his pastor and wife, and, of course, myself. It had taken us nearly two days to reach our destination in South Dakota. The trip lasted from July 27th to August 1st. As the long drive was progressing, I became homesick somewhat and began to worry whether or not this trip would gain me credible exposure. I began to feel better once I prayed and became acquainted better with Mr. Pierite's family. We rested at a hotel in Wichita, Kansas before continuing our drive to South Dakota. The Christian youth rally I was going to be speaking at was in South Dakota, but we stayed in a nice hotel in Valentine, Nebraska. During the trip, I did a great deal of praying to Jesus Christ, which strengthened me to a great deal. I did, however, feel a little agitated and discouraged somewhat during specific instances. The first was when I found out the program may have been canceled. The thought which entered my mind was enduring that long journey for nothing to be accounted for. I prayed for that to not happen, and thanks to Him that the rally did take place. I also became upset when we could not find the event location, but we did eventually, which was in thanks to Jesus Himself. Much time had endured after we arrived to the location, but the rally had not begun. I walked off and stood in the center of the sunshine just as mad as I could be.

I am person of progress and things being done on time. When these two things fail to happen at no fault of my own, I become worked up and aggravated. Some may consider this a major weakness, but I see it as tools used by God to mold me and make me stronger over time. My time for speaking was cut by ten minutes, but I realized God may have wanted me to speak for only ten minutes. The words I spoke came from Him directly, and I was passionately deeply in all the things I spoke. I felt better tremendously after speaking. I met and became very acquainted with the Christian rap artist who performed there. While he was very impressed with me for the books I have written, I was more inspired by the way God transformed his life. As the night progressed, I was filled with peace, joy, and hope. The next day was even better for me spiritually.

In addition to speaking at the Christian youth rally, I became great friends with Marshall Pierite's daughter and her friend. We visited Mount Rushmore, the statue of Crazy Horse, and the Wounded Knee Monument, which were all very interesting and worth seeing. We ate at places such as Pizza Hut, Applebee's, Ihop, and Texas Roadhouse. This trip to South Dakota was a very important thing that happened for me. Beside the fact I made some great new friends, I began to reaffirm the fullness of God's strength. I would begin again the work God has called me to do, which is make a difference in the lives of other people. I got closer to Jesus Christ than before, and my faith in Him reached a point that it had never reached before. The plague that existed inside of my mind came to an end, as well as my depression. All of the anger I felt for my ex-girlfriend had begun to leave, while feelings for my other ex had remained. However, I became strong enough to handle them and the temptations which followed. I entered an era of peace, joy, and consist spiritual growth; and I began assisting others with pressing issues in their lives. I began to post statuses on Facebook about consistent prayer, strong faith, leadership, and wisdom from God. I had taken all of the wonderful things God taught me and began to pass it onto everyone else. I also started doing a great deal of meditating, and I had once again the ability to focus on the things for which make my life what it has always consisted of. It became again my fundamental obligations to fulfill the journey God has set me upon, and to change the world for the better.

As time went by, I began to miss Avoyelles High School to a great deal. I did, however, maintain contact with many friends I had there. Many of them admire me greatly, and their friendship means very much to me. I made a promise to them that I would return to visit, and I would keep coming back until everyone was tired of seeing my face. The first time I visited was an unexpected one, even for me. Some of my friends had driven to my house without informing me they were coming. I went with them to hang out for the day. The date of this day was September 16th, 2012. As I saw that we were approaching Avoyelles High, I asked if we could visit the school. After running a short errand, we visited the school. It felt so wonderful to everyone again, and I vowed to make a second return. Next time, however, I wanted to do motivational speaking when I would go back. A month later, I visited Avoyelles High once again to ask the principal, Mr. Brent Whiddon, about setting a date and time for when I could speak to the Jr. High students. He said for me to call the school a couple of weeks when the Jr. High assembly was going to take place. I was very pleased by what I was told, and the date was the assembly was scheduled for was the exact same date I wanted in the beginning, which was November 2nd, 2012. I was also planning a bullying awareness fair for the entire public, which was scheduled for November 15th. I planned to speak to the Explorer's Club in regards to help for the program. I was told Club Day was the following week, so I came back then. It was the day after Election Day, November 7th, 2012, when I made a visit to Avoyelles High School.

I went back originally to speak to the Explorer's Club about the bullying awareness fair and to put up flyers with information about the program. However, I learned when I got to the school that Club Day was canceled, so I spoke to many classrooms throughout the school day. This went extremely well, and I knew it was God who aligned this day to take place the way it did. Something else that was very important would take place on this day. I expected to feel very excited about the re-election of President Barack Obama; however, this was very much different from what I was feeling. I experienced a political wake-up call, and I became very concerned for the future of our country. The feelings I had on this day were like never before, and the only thing I could wish for was Ronald Reagan to be our nation's leader once more. I really despised the fact that many people voted for the President to maintain their food stamps. Most importantly, I was dismayed greatly at how our country is moving further and further away from the principles for which have always made us strong and exceptional. I expressed my concerns with many people on this day. After everyone had gone home for the day, I sat on the concrete table near the walking track in front of the school. I said to Jesus Christ the very same words I said to Him for which changed my life for the better, only this time the words were referring to our country. I asked Jesus to give me the things to make the United States of America great again. On this day, November 7th, 2012, my deep aspiration for being the future leader of the United States became far more than for personal gain. It became solely about healing the crisis our nation endures, and inspiring hope and confidence in the hearts of the American people. From this day forward, I began praying for this and continuing to help lead others in the right direction.

I would go back to speak at Avoyelles High School one or two days each week for the following weeks. I spoke to the students about faith in God, believing in themselves, and leading a successful future. I also mentored a few individuals personally, which was very beneficial to them as well as me. After a couple of weeks, I had taken a break from speaking. I always enjoyed going to Avoyelles High to visit with old friends as well as speak to classes and mentor students. When I had gone back in a couple of weeks, it was to arrange speaking during for following week. The day did not carry out as expected; in fact, it was the worst day I had in a long time prior to that day. The date of this day was December 14th, 2012. If it were not for the strength of Jesus Christ, it would have gone much worse than it had done so. In addition to being told I could not interact with the kids while visiting, I learned of all the red tape in the Avoyelles Parish School system. Many of the regulations the teachers have to follow are very demoralizing and discouraging. All of this was pushing very well talented, decent, and hardworking teachers out of the system. Those teachers who would remain in the system would not have the ability to enjoy what they do everyday. The individuals who would end up suffering the most are the students at absolutely no fault of their own. The regulations consist of federal, state, and local control. Teachers are being told how to teach their students, and the discipline system is based on sympathy rather than what is best for everyone in general. There are many other issues I learned of for which need to be addressed before we reach the point of no return.

All I could think of were all of my friends in school who are suffering, and how much of their futures are at high stake. Much throughout the day, I kept saying to myself that there is a crisis that needs to be dealt with and a school system for which needs to be changed heavily. As angry as I had become of this, it became worse when they attempted to stifle me from visiting with and helping friends at school and regulate my speaking there. It was beginning to become more and more evident that those in charge of the school system not only snubbed at motivation for the students, but does not care about the students and their future. As I arrived home, I was very upset and frustrated because of the system as well as that particular day itself. I learned shortly of the terrible shooting massacre at Sandy Hook Elementary School in Newtown, Connecticut. I became so worked up inside that I needed to go for a walk. I went for a bite to eat at a fast-food restaurant near my house. Feeling terrible for all of those affected by the shooting, I prayed heavily for the families and the souls of the children who were killed. As I was walking back home, I called my best friend from school, Larry Martin. I told him how I felt, as he felt much the same as I. He said to me that I am the one to change all of that which is wrong. He told me also that I will change the world, which inspired me very much. When I arrived home, I called Mr. Scotty Dauzat and told him about the day I had. He said he would keep me in prayer, and I promised the same for him and his family.

Afterwards I began listening to music as I meditated on making things better for the future. The only benefit I received from the events on this day was an increase in my burning flame to bring about a change. I was tested on this day to great extent, and it was Jesus Christ who maintained my restraint from lashing our and/or giving in. The fundamental issue I aspired to tackle was the education system, and I pledged my life and career to do so. As I began to pray about this, all of the frustration and anger was transformed into motivation to do what I love, which is help make people's lives better. I remember being told by a very good friend of mine that the best way to make the school system better is to be centered in one place instead of being scattered all over the place. Moreover, she told me I needed to be in the system in order to bring about legitimate, long-term changes. After much thinking and prayer, I decided to apply for a substitute teacher position at Avoyelles High School for the second semester. There are many teachers who had planned to quit teaching, and it was in my heart to acquire one of those positions to ensure that some of the students would learn whatever they needed to know. The following week I went to the school board office and obtained a substitute teacher application. I went to Avoyelles High School the next day to talk about it to the principal.

It was stated on the application that the age limit to be a substitute teacher was twenty-one, but I was told school board officials it was actually eighteen. The other qualifications included a high-school education and a clean criminal record. As I was awaiting to be called to substitute at school, I called the school board office to check whether or not if Avoyelles High School received my information. I was told then I was ineligible to be substitute teacher because they learned the true age limit was in fact twenty-one. I attempted to make multiple efforts to see if I could still take the position, but the desire to be a substitute teacher would soon be faded from my heart. Instead I made it my obligation to focus more on myself and getting into college during the Fall semester in 2013. I was accepted in Louisiana College in Pineville, Louisiana. I will major in political science and minor, most likely, in history. I anticipate on transferring in a couple of years to larger universities and colleges such as Morehouse, American, and Stanford. There is a strong chance that I will attend law school after four or six years of college. I have intentions of becoming a school teacher and college instructor. My ultimate desire to pursue a successful political career, and I will use it for the betterment of our nation's future.

All that you can possibly imagine has happened in my life. I have been betrayed,, heartbroken, rejected, criticized, and castigated. I have struggled, sacrificed, and bled emotionally. It was all in the name of my Life, Lord and Savior, and I overcame it all through His grace and long-term strength. I would not be where I am if it were not for Jesus Christ. As I have always said, I am on a journey to achieve profound greatness not only for my life, but for the world. All of the gifts God has given me are to affect the lives of others in a positive aspect. I have always been very unique in the eyes of other people, and I prefer much to be this way. There is absolutely nothing that could ever possible be said or done to destroy me or make me think less of the person who God created me to be. I am deeply grateful to my Lord God Jesus Christ for making me the person I am and for who I will become over the years to come. It is upon Him where my life rests, and all the things that were overcame were done by He who lives in me. I continue to make it my top priority to give my family in the future the things

I never had and was forced to struggle for. The only things that are important now are maintaining my relationship with Jesus Christ, obtaining the best education, giving my future wife and children a prosperous life, and ensuring that the world is much better off by the time my journey on Earth has been fulfilled.

> No weapon formed against you shall prosper; and every tongue that rises against you in judgment, you shall condemn. This is the heritage of the servants of the Lord. Isaiah 54:17

> Be strong and have good courage: be not afraid nor be dismayed; for the Lord thy God is with you wherever you shall journey. Joshua 1:7

Chapter 4

MY WALK WITH CHRIST

There are always those times when people ask me for the reason that I remain joyful and peace on a consistent basis. When I asked this, I cannot help but to think about all of the times when I ask others for their reasons. I remember the day when I was attending one of my best friend's graduation party. For most of that day, I was feeling extremely vulnerable and upset. It was because I became difficult for my then-girlfriend and myself to see each other when we wanted. My friend's uncle, who was present during the party, helped me feel better to a certain extent. He and I discussed politics for a short while, and I informed him of the books I had written. However, I could not help the way I was feeling, so I asked my friend's uncle a very simple question, expecting a simple answer. I asked him how could I become happy and peaceful again. He said for me to go to the rock, which is Jesus Christ. I had known this previously to a great extent due to the faith I have always had in Christ, but I was looking for a snap-of-the-finger solution. Eventually I would grow stronger from this day, while there have been times such as these before and after. I have always recovered from every emotional and mental downfall for which I have experienced.

Many situations have overwhelmed me heavily at times, but I always rose above and beyond. The reason I am able to do this and remain full of peace and joy is that I choose to center my life around a strong foundation in Jesus Christ, which is everlasting and cannot be compromised. This enables me to bounce back up immediately from every fall I take. Many people base their lives upon things that are temporary and things such as relationships, money, and other material items. There is nothing wrong with having these things; in fact, all of us desire them at some points in time during our lives. However, if there is no strong spiritual foundation at the core of our hearts, life becomes more difficult without many of those things we desire. The foundation that is the center of my life is faith in Jesus Christ. I have had this faith in Christ for years, along with a deep, passionate love for Him. Jesus

Christ entered my life and did what no man or woman could ever reverse, which is reveal to me the gift He has stored inside of me to be the person He created me to be. This enables me to live a great and wonderful life that is full of the riches that any person could ever ask for. When I am experiencing hardship and instability, I pray to Him for the way forward as He leads me there in time. While experiencing times of excitement and great joy, I remember who strengthens me to do so and praise God heavily for making me who I am. The thing I always keep in mind is that my life is a journey, which has been pre-ordained by God Himself. He has me on to fulfill His purpose for the world and lead others in a positive direction on His behalf.

I was once a person who would worry about things consistently, doubted His ability as well as my own, and feared all the time for the worst. Jesus Christ took this person and changed his life for the better. He took all that was wrong inside of him and removed them forever. Jesus revealed His greatness inside of me and made me the strongest for which I have ever been, while strengthening me continuously along the way. The things that other people may say and do fail to discourage me and do not make me think less of who God created me to be. While I am deeply grateful to be who and where I am, I realize that God has far greater things in store for the future. He will build upon the things in my life that He has already done. My faith is at the point where if I am in pain, Jesus Christ will heal it simply if I ask Him to do so. Through constant prayer and a strong commitment to the Lord God Jesus Christ, I will reach the fullness of the prosperity and greatness that is in store.

Vision Shaped by Faith

Ever since Jesus Christ has come into my life, He has been transforming me into a much wiser, better person. My broad perspective of the world has shifted to more of a deep spiritual aspect. I had little knowledge of the tremendous things that God could do in my life before I asked Him to make it great. When I was much younger, I had no true vision of what the world could become. I found myself trying constantly to align with the views of others, politically. When I would write and give speeches, I always did my best to be exactly like other great political leaders. I was as if I was an empty vessel that was lost and unsure of who I really was from deep within. As time went on, I began to receive a tremendous deal of wisdom that I had never known and thought of before. All of that for which I began to learn did not come from any books, persons, and other earthly sources. I knew strongly in my heart that every bit of knowledge was coming from God directly. Since it came from Him directly, it was to be transported to other people so their lives could be affected in a positive manner. This led me to the belief that there is something called direct wisdom, which is called divine wisdom also. Direct wisdom is given to an individual from God directly to perform the duties He called him or her to perform. Also, indirect wisdom is learned or received from an earthly source, which can come from God also.

My vision of the world is centered around the principle that each and every human being has a gift from God inside of them for which was given to him or her at birth. All of us were given this gift to fulfill the will and promise of God, which is to make the world a better place for those to come after. God created us all in His image, which makes us all beautiful and unique. He knew how each of us would look and consist of before we were brought into the world because He pre-ordained for us to be a certain way. Because God made us who we are, there is absolutely nothing wrong with who we are. The only things that may become wrong are those that which we create such as standards, judgments, and criticisms that are based on race, religion, gender, and, most importantly, physical appearance. Since it was God who made us all a certain way, all standards and judgments and criticisms that are based on these things are not only illegitimate, but they stand against God and the plan He intends for us. You and I are equal in the eyes of our Lord God no matter who we are and where we come from, and He loves us all more than we could ever imagine. Every person has the God-given opportunity and God-given ability to achieve profound greatness on behalf God, themselves, and many others. This can be accomplished through strong faith in Him and persistent determination. I consider these principles at the forefront of my life, and I emphasize them in all writings and when speaking to students, church congregations, and all others.

I became convinced increasingly that the spiritual vision that is in my heart was not in line with my views on how government should work in people's lives. In the beginning of 2011, I became passionately against issues such as abortion, same-sex marriage, and embryonic stem cell research. These three things are not only immoral and wrong heavily in the eyes of God, but lead individuals further and further away from the greatness that God has in store. When I saw the things God has done in my life, I could not help but imagine the wonderful things He could do for others. All of the things that God does in the life of a person will affect the lives of others. This is what led me to the fundamental truth that abortion is a form of murder and a grave threat to all human life on this planet. When I see pictures of me when I was an infant child, I am thankful to God for all that He has done as I realize that my life could have ended before it was realized. As I see my nieces and nephews, I could never help but to wonder how and why anyone would support and advocate for something has cold-hearted and cruel as abortion. No child should die because his or her mom, who may have been irresponsible and careless, does not feel the need or desire to carry him or her for nine months. However, all of the women who have been involved in a negative situation should be prayed for and assisted by those around them. The worst mistake that you or I could make is to judge, castigate, and degrade those who have been hurt and need help. No one should have the right or ability to end the life of any other that is of no threat to his or her life. If you are a believer or supporter of abortion, I ask you this simple question: what if you were in a position where your life was going to end and there was absolutely nothing that you or anyone could do to prevent? Later on throughout the course of my career, I will use every force I have in the strength of Jesus Christ to rid abortion from the face of this Earth so that every person is preserved the right to experience God's wonderful gifts and what the world has to offer.

As for same-sex marriage, I believe in what the Holy Bible says about homosexuality itself. Leviticus 18:22 states firmly, "You shall not lie with a male as with a woman. It is an abomination." In verses 24-26 it states, "do not defile yourselves with any of these things; for by all these the nations are defiled, which I am casting out before you. 'For the land is defiled; therefore, I visit the punishment of its iniquity upon it, and the land vomits out its inhabitants. 'You shall therefore keep My statutes and My judgments, and shall not commit any of these abominations, either any of your own nation or any stranger who dwells among you." I was once a supporter of the choice to for an individual to marry someone of the same sex. As my relationship with Jesus Christ was growing, I began to question myself about this position. I had to decide if I was going to stand up for God's word or find reasons to align my position with those of others. Even while I would not be affected by the marriage of another couple, I would not support under any circumstances anything for which God says is wrong. However, I do not judge anyone who does obey God's word. As a follower of Jesus Christ, I believe in the phrase that goes "Love the sinner. Hate the sin." This does not mean promote sin, but instead to fight against. If someone is doing wrong, I have a duty as a Christian to tell him or her the truth about what they are doing. I have also an obligation to not say things and perform actions that would encourage the individual to act against God. This would make me an accomplice of sin. It would be wrong for me in the eyes of God to say I believe in His word personally but support that of which He says is wrong. God says that homosexuality is wrong, and same-sex marriage only encourages people further to go along and be homosexual. As a Christian, I am obligated by God to stand up for what is morally just in His eyes. If God says all of us are to love one another, it would not be an act of love if I say and do things to encourage others to go against God and His word. It was wrong spiritually for President Obama to declare his support for same-sex marriage because of his daughters support it. It was in his duty as a Christian to not only stand up for God's Word, but explain to his daughters the truth of what God says about homosexuality and the principles of marriage. For it says in James 5:19-20, "Brethren, if anyone among you wanders from the Truth, and someone turns him back, let him know that he who turns a sinner from the error of his way will save a soul from death (Hell) and cover a multitude of sins." I will always stand up for the Lord God Jesus Christ and His solemn commands. Through the strength of Him, I will help many of those who are going down the wrong path to learn the Truth by finding themselves in Jesus Christ. As it regards to the issue of embryonic stem-cell research, I stand in strong opposition. No person should take away the things that an individual needs to live a stable, productive lifestyle. God is the One who provided every man and woman the vital elements for which he or she needs to live, and they should not be taken away by anyone under any circumstances.

Imagine if you were in a position of where you had the power to end abortion, same-sex marriage, and embryonic stem-cell research. You know already that God Himself says that all of these things are wrong. As a follower of the Lord God Jesus Christ, would you choose to follow Him and rid the world of these things He Himself says are wrong? Or would you choose to follow the world and allow these things to happen? You cannot be of God and the world at the same time.

For some time now, there has been a major debate in our country about gun violence and whether or not we need more laws to prevent crime and tragedy plagued by gun violence. All of us know what the two arguments advocate for. One side believes that all guns should be banned from the practice of ownership, while the other side believes that more guns are needed for protection from an outside attempt of attack. From my perspective, there should be a third choice. What if you are in a position where you do not have any physical means of protection from a possible attack? The best possible source of protection you could ever have is the ultimate faith in Jesus Christ. With the ultimate faith in Him, there is no need for a gun for protection. You are perfectly fine as long as you have your gun by side, but it will not do you any good if you no longer have it. God can put a realm of protection around you and those you love if you ask Him to do, and you must not doubt in His ability to keep you and your loved ones safe from harm. If I am ever asked if I am in favor of guns or not, I will say simply that I am in favor of God's source of protection for my life and those I love with all of my heart. I love the Lord with all of my heart and have the ultimate faith in Him, and I trust Him to be there for me always. There is not a time when you do not need God's protection; for every second of time is a blessing from Him. God can protect you not only from physical harm by others, but from every force of evil sent your way from Satan himself.

As for economic and financial concerns, I went from a secular, liberal perspective to a view that is not only conservative, but parallel with what pleases God and brings individuals and the world closer to Him in the long-term. There are many who believe that government should be either the dominant or a strong force in people's lives and should take from those who are successful and re-distribute that wealth among those who are not as successful. I believe that this is entirely the wrong way to help strengthen individuals and help them realize God's gifts inside of them, and it goes against the principle that God blesses us so that others can be blessed and lifted. All of those who may be in poverty and despair have different circumstances. There are some who choose to not work and do anything to put themselves in a better situation, while these individuals cannot be helped by others. By that same token, there are those who require assistance and are doing everything they can to be in a better situation.

What is happening in our country is that those in government, liberal Democrats particularly, treats many as if they are victims. They seek to convince individuals that the problems in their lives are at the fault of others, which could not be further from the truth than where it is. They insist also on putting labels on individuals based upon their circumstances such as poor, middle-class, and wealthy. This puts a mental cap on how much these individuals will achieve in their lifetime. The only labels that people have are those for which God gives them, and all persons can achieve as much as their God-given talents will take them. Liberal Democrats believe also that those who are wealthier and more successful than others should be punished for achieving greatness in their lives. If you were blessed with something you have always wanted in life, which could be anything you have ever dreamed of, how would you feel if it was taken away from you at no fault of your own? I am not sure about you, but I would feel as if all of the things I may have had to do to achieve it would have been for nothing. I would feel also as if I will not work as hard to obtain the desires in my heart because I will always know there is a chance that all of them could be taken away. All of those who are beneath others in some aspects should be helped in a way that would bring them closer to realizing their potential. This can be achieved through a strong insistence on faith in Jesus Christ, themselves, and what can be accomplished. I tell young people all the time that each of them has the opportunity to lead the best, most successful lives within their capacity. They will never achieve this as long as we have a government and society that leads them further and further from dependence on God to a secular source such as government.

As I think about what God has done in my life, and as I envision the future with my wife and kids, all of this becomes very personal for me. I know deep in my heart the kind of world I desire to leave behind after my journey on this Earth is complete, and the type of government we have is seeking the contrary. Most liberals who are in positions of power and whom I know are not true believers in Jesus Christ, do not have faith in the limitless possibilities of Him, and do not follow biblical principles. I have made it my fundamental obligation to help people realize their God-given talents and abilities and to understand the true meaning of limitless faith in the wonderful things possible in the future. I have also make it my duty to end all of the things that lead our country and society down a negative path. I realize this journey will be difficult to accomplish, as I will face great opposition from the enemy (the devil) and his followers. I believe, however, in the calling God has voiced in my heart. I have the ultimate faith that He will strengthen me to the end and see me there.

> I can do all things through Christ who strengthens me. Philippians 4:13
> If anyone is in Christ; he is a new creation; the old has gone, the new has come! 2 Corinthians 5:17

Chapter 5

A JOURNEY IN FAITH

I can remember being a much younger boy and in the stage where I questioned many of the things around me. I would question absolutely anything and everything I did not understand. It was the time in my life where some things would be left unclear when explained to me. While some things would be simple to understand, I learned there are other things I would need to understand fully through experience. I always felt it is best this way because you would have a testimony to tell to others, which can help them learn clearly what certain things mean. From my perspective, learning some things the difficult way is better because it can possibly make you stronger and wiser in the long-term if you allow it to. There are many instances in which this would be applied in my life such as rejection, vulnerability, and failure. Each and every experience that applied to these situations set me on a higher path in the long-term. I would not be the person I am if it were not for all that I had experienced. The most important thing I have learned in my life is what it means to have faith. Faith is the greatest thing that any man or woman could ever have, but he or she cannot have it until he or she learns its true meaning and experience it over time for his—or herself.

DEFINING FAITH

There are many who believe that faith and religion are the same. While the both are connected in some manner, they are distinctly different from each other. Religion is primarily man-made and has been manipulated by many over time to fit what is more acceptable to them. There is a great number of people who pretend to have a relationship with Jesus Christ by attending church regularly and by presenting themselves to others a certain way. However, they do not behave upon that of Christ nor live up to His principles. While they profess to be followers of Christ, they believe and act upon the things that He stands in opposition with. For example, they may hold deep-seated prejudices of certain kinds of people, they may talk negatively of others on a consistent basis, or they may even be skeptical or cynical in general. People like this seek to always justify their actions, which goes against God's Word heavily, with human logic and understanding. While all of us are imperfect and make mistakes, we are all obligated to reach out to God in an effort to grow closer to Him. We should admit to Him as well as ourselves our weaknesses and ask God to strengthen us along the way. From my perspective, the only things religion seeks to accomplish are judging those who may be different and condemning people who commit acts of sin. Religionists say often that those who have not accepted Jesus Christ are going to Hell. All of this do nothing but manipulate the truth of Jesus Christ and push genuine, open-minded individuals away from learning what the truth really is.

At this moment, I ask that you forget all things you may have heard about faith, until you are done reading and understanding this chapter. Faith, for me, has always been the center of my life. Everything I believe and strive for in my life is based upon the faith I have in the Lord God Jesus Christ. I am able to live in abundant joy, peace, hope, and stability, all of which is based upon what the future holds in store. Because I have faith, I am able to see the light in every dark moment on my journey. I thank God humbly for helping me understand what it means to have an ultimate faith in Him. As I write and speak to others about faith is, it is based solely on how my own life has been affected for the better. I have seen what faith has done on my behalf, and I have made it a duty to help make faith clear to all of those in the world who are unclear to its true meaning. Faith is the following:

A) It is Knowing that God has placed on a journey to fulfill His will and purpose, which is to bring about profound greatness into the world we all live in.

B) It is Knowing that God is in total control of your life and everything that happens in it.

C) It is Trusting God and Knowing that He will bring about the desires of your heart because He is the One who stored them deep within you.

D) It is Knowing that everything in your life will carry out exactly the way it should on the perfect timing.

All things that are the opposite of these principles such as constant worry, doubt, and fear do not resemble that of faith. It is normal on few occasions where we are uncertain about various things that are heavily critical. These are perfect opportunities for us to reach out to Jesus Christ for strength. If you have strong faith, you will search always for the best in all things that happen. When you lose in competition, you realize that God ha something better in store and seek to become stronger to achieve better things in the future. If someone says or does wrong to you, you acknowledge that something must be wrong or unclear in that person's life that must be dealt with by God, which will enable you to forgive that individual. You will pray for persons like that heavily and help them become better persons in the eyes of God. A strong, committed faith in accordance to the principles stated above can be achieved if you simply asked Jesus Christ to come into your life and change it forever. Once you ask Him, you must stay committed to Him through prayer and following His commands.

THE PROCESS OF FAITH

If you are at a certain point in your life for which you wish to not be, you will be inspired to envision yourself living in great prosperity and stability in every aspect of your existence. You may have experienced constant rejection or heartbreak due to cruelty from others and past relationships, respectively. I have had a great deal of experience with all of these throughout my journey. With strong, unwavering faith, you are able to realize that God will not only reward you with great, lasting friendships, but He will unite you with the man or woman that you will spend the rest of your life with. When it comes to major, complex issues within your community and the world, through faith you will not only have hope for what can and should be achieve, but you will be empowered to solve the problem with your gifts from God. While having faith can be a choice, it is more of a process that must be endured. Faith is not given to you, but it is sought and worked for through persistence and humility. It is your responsibility entirely to decide whether or not you will obtain faith in Jesus Christ. The process begins when you ask God to make it clear to you along the way. God will bring you through difficult situations to make you more equipped to do His work. He will never give you more than you can handle under any circumstances. The fact that you may be experiencing difficulty is evident in itself that you are able to overcome what is before you. God knows how strong you are because He created you in His image. He does not bring you through hard times to see how strong you are, but for you to realize for yourself what you are capable of. God knew who you would become before He conceived you into your mother's womb. He loves you deeply and unconditionally, as He will never abandon you under any circumstances.

God will bring you to the fire, but will never choose to leave you there. You are the one who chooses to stay there if you do. God may allow you also to even bring yourself into difficult situations to set you on a better path. God can take all of that for which is negative and transform them into positive. It will be all of the things that God allows to happen in your life that offer the greatest opportunity for your faith in Him to excel beyond your imagination. Whether or not you utilize your opportunity is entirely your choice to pursue the process. It is not the situations or the magnitude of them, but how you deal with them. It is a whether or not you will react with a positive mindset, and strive to live better and achieve more; for faith is based not on ability but attitude.

You may have decided to not learn about faith and how to achieve it for yourself. You may have decided the most important things in your life are the safety and well-being of your family as well as yourself. As a person of great faith in Jesus Christ, I ask you to think thoroughly of where you are in your life. Are you enjoying life to the fullest? Do you have peace and stability? Do you have many of the things you have longed desired for? Before you answer these questions inside of your mind, think about them deeply. As you think about these things, disregard everything you may have heard about religion and church. Faith is not as complicated as you may have thought it was. Instead, it is the sole engine to living a great and wonderful life. All you must do is ask God to come down into your life and change it for the better. It will be a process, but once you finally make it there, you will have a faith in the Lord God Jesus Christ that can never be wavered or compromised no matter what happens. With the ultimate faith in Jesus Christ, you will not only overcome all obstacles and achieve every desires, but you will able to lift others and help lead them to great new heights that were never, ever anticipated. More importantly, you can finally be the person that God created you to be with no shame or doubt in who you are with no fear or worry for what you can and must achieve for the future.

Seek your happiness in the Lord, and He will give your heart's desire. Psalm 37:4

The Lord will fight for you; you need to be still. Exodux 14:14

Have faith in God. What I am about to tell you is true. Suppose one of you says to the mountain, "Go and throw yourself into the sea." You must not doubt in your heart. You must believe that what you saw will happen. Then it will be done for you. So I tell you, when you pray for something, believe that you have already received it. Then it will be yours. And when you stand praying, forgive anyone you have anything against. Then your Father in Heaven will forgive your sins. Matthew 11:22-26

Have I commanded you? Be strong and have good courage; be not afraid, nor be dismayed; for the Lord thy God is with you wherever you shall journey. Joshua 1:9

Ask, and it shall be given to you; seek, and you shall find; knock, and it shall be opened unto. Matthew 7:7-8

Trust in the Lord with all of your heart. Never rely on what you think you know. Remember the Lord in everything you do, and He will show you the right way. Never let yourself think you are, simply obey the Lord and refuse to do wrong. Proverbs 3:5-7

God is our shelter and strength, always ready to help in times of trouble. So we will not be afraid, even if the Earth is shaken and mountains fall into the oceans depths; even if seas roar and rage, and the hills are shaken by violence. Psalm 46:1-3

I will not leave you until I have done what I have promised you. Genesis 28:15

Do not worry about anything, but pray about everything. With a thankful heart offer up to your prayers and requests to God. Then because you belong to Christ Jesus, God will bless you with peace that no one can understand completely. And this peace will control the way you think and feel. Phillipians 4:6-7 Be strong and courageous. Do not be afraid or terrified because of them, for the Lord your God goes with you; He will never leave nor forsake you. Deuteronomy 31:6

So do not fear, for I am with you; do not be dismayed, for I am your God. I will strength you and help you. Isaiah 41:10

Therefore, my dear brothers and sisters, stand firm. Let nothing move you. Always give yourselves fully to the work of the Lord, because you know that your labor in the Lord is not in vain. Corinthians 15:58

Chapter 6

DISCOVERING YOU AND YOUR PURPOSE

Was there ever a day in your life when you asked yourself questions such as "why am I living? What causes me to wake up every morning? Why am I here?" What are things that enter your mind after you ask yourself these small questions? There are probably many different things you may think of, but the best thing to do would be to find out for yourself what the true answers are. It is a fact that you are here of us are for a specific reason, no matter what who you are. There are times in your life when you feel discouraged or experience disappointments, which may have led you to feel as if you wanted to live no longer. You may have also been judged, criticized, or rejected on many occasions, which may have made you feel worthless or unwanted. It is situations such as these that lead many individuals to not enjoy life as the days go by. This also makes it harder for people to enjoy life to the fullest and make it the best as possible for themselves and others. All of us have felt this way before in our lives, but it is how we deal with our situation that is most important. We can choose to be negative about ourselves and focus on what may be wrong; or we can be positive about our situation and strive for peace, stability, and joy in the long-term. You are worth far more than all of the criticisms you may receive. All of the negative things that you may have experienced do not have to keep in a situation where you wish to not be. It is your responsibility to obtain the long-term strength from Jesus Christ to live a great life and learn your purpose for being brought into the world. It is a process that is not promised to be short and simple, but you can achieve your purpose fully if you are committed to doing so.

YOUR JOURNEY: DEFINING YOU AND YOUR PURPOSE THROUGH JESUS CHRIST

There are always those times when things do not end in the way we would have liked them to. We may experience many situations that bring great adversity, pain, and disappointment. May of us have had unsuccessful relationships; we have lost a family member or a great friend, lost in competition, and have dealt with the evilness and cruelty of other people. There are also many other situations that you, I, and others have experienced. Most of the time we week to figure out the reasons for things that happened to us, and sometimes wish for an outcome different from the one that happened actually. You may not know or even believe it, but each and every person is on a journey. Every human being born into the world has been placed by God on his or her own journey. Each person's journey is different from those of others, and they have been pre-ordained by God Himself. Some of the things that may take place in your life may seem too dramatic to handle. However, God allows many of these things to happen to make us stronger and lead to a specific and better outcome in the future.

God may use an obstacle to detour you from what you may have anticipated to accomplish so that you can achieve something better than what you planned originally. For example, you may have intentions of competing in a talent show at your school or in your neighborhood. Your ultimate goal is to succeed in winning first place, which is what you should always strive to achieve. You worked diligently for a month in preparation to give the best performance that anyone has yet to hear. For the entire time until the talent show, you feel deep within your heart as if you will win first place with absolutely no ounce of doubt. Instead you place either lower or not at all. You are overwhelmed with great disappointment and discouragement for a period time. However, you take some time to improve the lyrics in your song and practice singing it until you become better and better. One day you are either talking with some friends or in school. All of a sudden, you ask if you could practice your song in front of everyone. After doing so, everyone is impressed greatly with your performance. In fact, one person asks if you would like to perform your song at his or her church. After doing so, you are requested to sing at additional churches. Then you begin to grow in popularity and receive commission for every time you perform. As your audience grows, you will be speaking to crowds filled with prominent individuals. You are discovered by an agent and will soon become famous throughout the country, with great intentions to expand worldwide. The best, most important aspect of the entire situation is that you are now in a position where you can inspire millions of people and make a difference in the lives of those people through your music as well as your personal story. This is only one example of many stories such as this one.

Every disappointment and downfall will always lead to something so much better than expected in the beginning. This is exactly how God works in our lives to bring about His greatness. All of the things that take place during our journey were designed in the way of one thing leading to something greater. God knows who you are and what you are capable. Therefore, He would never bestow upon you more than you can handle. All things that have happened in your life are within your ability to overcome, and you should thank God that things are not worst than what they are.

The journey God has placed you on is to achieve profound greatness on behalf of yourself and the world itself. You are here on Earth to help change the lives of others in a positive manner and to simply help people. If you fulfill these obligations, many lives would be transformed greatly by the time your journey is complete. God is the only One who decides when your journey is complete, but it will not be until you have done all of the things He has called you to do. While God will always be available through prayer, realizing and completing the things He has called you to do will require listening to His voices inside of your heart.

In an effort to fulfill your journey, God has stored greatness deep within you. You are the one who is responsible for realizing that greatness inside of you. You are able to help others live better because of what God has done in your life. The way you help people is by sharing with them what God has done on your behalf and showing them the way to receive Him into their lives. God's greatness within you is exemplified through your gifts, your uniqueness, and your personality, which are all divine. All of these are the things needed not only to fulfilling your journey, but to live a great, wonderful life. So the questions that must be answered are the following: how must you realize God's gifts inside of you and what makes you unique? How can these things truly make the world a better place? The process begins with developing a relationship with Jesus Christ. Jesus Christ will reveal to your gifts and give you the strength to be the person He created you to be. Then you will begin to believe in and admire yourself for who you are truly, and it will no longer be about becoming what the world expects you to become. As I stated earlier, this process may not be as short or easy as you may want it to be. Everything will depend on not only your ability to keep moving forward, but your attitude.

A RELATIONSHIP WITH JESUS CHRIST

The most important thing you can and should have in your life is a strong, deep, and committed relationship with the Lord God Jesus Christ. You may have heard the story of Christ sacrificing His life on the Cross of Calvary and being risen to Heaven three days later. This is what gave each and every person the opportunity for his or her sins to be forgiven so they could enter the Kingdom of Heaven. It is this story that should encourage you to accept Jesus Christ as your Life, Lord and Savior. There are many other reasons you should acknowledge Him as the leader of your life. One of them is having a spiritual realm of protection from evils in the world such as temptation, immorality, and the harmful intentions of certain kinds of people. There has probably been many times in your life when you may have been attacked by others in various ways, or have been tempted to do things that bring great danger and major consequences. The situation could consist of anything you may think of. God's hedge of realm of protection ensures us peace, safety, and stability. There are many times when we ask God to not allow certain things to happen to us or for certain people to not be around us. God does not work this way all of the time. Instead He allows us to experience risky situations to mold us and make us stronger and wiser. When bad situations bring us down, God will always be there to lift you and guide you on forward.

We live in a world of great challenge and tribulation, but Jesus Christ seeks to strengthen you to deal with it all because He loves you far more than you could ever imagine. Having a relationship with Jesus Christ is important also because He not only loves you and cares for you deeply, but He believes in you and what you are capable of. When we think of how our parents always did their best to protect us from hard as we were much younger. It is because they cared about us with all of their hearts, and they were not sure of what would happen to us if we did wrong and/or were left in a difficult or risky situation. The only difference with Jesus Christ is that He knows truly the source of your inner abilities because He sees what is inside of you. He knows what is in your heart, mind, and soul. Since Jesus believes in you, He allows you to experience difficulty and hardship. He may allow your relationship or friendship with a certain person to end terribly. He may allow you to endure ridicule and criticisms. He may even allow you to lose someone or something that meant a great deal to you. All of these things happen because Jesus knows that you can overcome these situations, and He is seeking to lead you to bigger and better things beyond your own expectations. He promises also to strengthen you through your struggle if you stay committed to Him. The fundamental goal is to bring you closer to Jesus Christ so you can fulfill the plan He has for your life. The questions that must be answered now are the following: what does it means to have a relationship with Jesus Christ? How can you have one and strengthen it over time?

In my own life, God has always reigned highly superior. Even as a little kid I never doubted His existence. As I became a teenager, I began to pray more often and develop a faith in Jesus Christ. While I do attend church consistently, I did not always do so. I would attend a church service every other week or once or twice a month. I was not raised in a particular church, which is most likely why I did not attend regularly as I was growing up. From personal experience, church never played a major role in helping me develop my relationship with Jesus Christ as well as my faith in Him. When many of us hear the word *church*, we think physical building, a pastor, religion, etc. The word *church* as referenced in scripture refers to all of the people who have committed their lives and hearts to serving Christ. What we refer to as church on Sundays or any other days of the week is only a gathering of individuals who should love God and stand committed to Him in all aspects of his or her life. To have a relationship with Jesus Christ, you must love Him with all of your heart, acknowledge Him in every area of your life, and reach out to Him in prayer for courage, joy, and peace. It means to give full thanks to Him for everything you have in your life and will have later on. When you are feeling as great as ever, you will humble yourself before Jesus Christ. This means to not feel as if you no longer need

Him just because things are going in your favor. Also, when you are down or in a situation where you do not want to be, you should ask Christ to heal your pain and lift you up. This will give you hope for the future and eventually set you free from your situation. There are those times when you will question many things that happen in your life. Your questions may be left unanswered for an extended period of time, but this is only part of God's plan. As Christ leads you in your journey, however, you will begin to figure out the reasons for certain things that had taken place. You will also become grateful eternally that things progressed in a particular manner due to where you have reached.

You may be experiencing difficulty and pain at this very moment and are desiring to feel better. God promises to lead you forward if you rest aside all worries, negative thoughts and feelings, and even the blame game. God cannot work for the better in your life if you resort to anger, bitterness, and negativity. The prayers you send to Him moves the power of Him in your life. Your personal relationship with Him belongs to you and Jesus Christ, and He will commit to you for as long as you commit to Him. There is absolutely no man or woman who will be able step between you and Jesus, unless you allow them to do so. All you must do to develop a relationship with Christ is ask Him simply to come into your life and make it great. It has absolutely nothing to do with your race, religion, sexual orientation, circumstances, or anything related. No matter who you are and where you are in your journey, Jesus can change your life forever and make it greater than you could ever expect. At this moment, I ask that you consider where you have been, where you are, and where you desire to go. Determine yourself that you are ready to lead a new type of life, and commit yourself to doing just that. You can have this through a relationship with the Lord God Jesus Christ. The only thing you must do now is say to Him these simple words: Lord Jesus Christ, please help me get the tools and resources I need to put my life on the road to long-term prosperity. In time after you do this, He will reach back down to you and do many things on your behalf that you never, ever imagined!

You and Your Purpose

Have you ever taken the time to wonder why you were made the way you are? All of us have done this at one point or another in our lives. Each of us wonder sometimes why we may look a particular way or why our voices may sound a certain way. We even seek to understand why we were born to a certain family or in a certain neighborhood, city, or country. While it is normal to have concerns such as these out of curiosity, the best thing you can do is to simply ask God for the reason and He will be more than glad to reveal it to you at the right time. You may not be satisfied with the way you were created. You may not like the way your face is structured or other things related. You may be one of those persons who wish you were either a totally different way or living not at all. There are millions of individuals across the world who feel this way, and it will be only a matter of time before a breaking point is reached. I was once at the point in my life where I was dissatisfied with who I thought I was. I did not believe in myself, I did not feel any sense of purpose for being alive, and I felt even as if I was ugly and unattractive. I would not even look in the mirror. It was Jesus Christ who revealed to me the truth of who I am and why He made me the way I am. You were created by God in His image, and He knew exactly what He was doing as He was creating you. God knows each of us and what we would consist of long before conception. God is the One who made us who we are, and we exist just as we should.

There is absolutely nothing wrong with you, other than the many misled allusions created by your mind and other people. You are beautiful and unique in the eyes of God just as you are, and you have many attributes that others do not have; for each of us are different from one another. Each of us have many great things inside of us, which come from God, to give to the world. These great things inside of you gives you the potential to change lives and help make the world a better place for our children and grandchildren. You were put here to make a difference in the lives of others and bring glory to God's name. This is your fundamental purpose for being brought into the world. All individuals were put here to do these things. In order to these things, God has stored certain abilities, talents, and desires deep within you. The means for which you would fulfill your purpose may be fundamentally different from those of others. In other words, everyone is different from each other and have different gifts from God. There are many different ways God may have enabled you to work on His behalf, but it is you who are responsible for learning what your God-given gifts are.

So the question that must be answered at this point is the following: how must you learn of the things God gave you to fulfill His purpose for your life? From personal experience, I learned of the many gifts inside of me by reaching out to Jesus Christ through prayer and simple conversation. I asked Him to help me get the things to make my life great, and He taught me soon that I already have them. The only thing that was left to do was be revealed to what they are. It was not very long before Christ did just that. I was already a motivational speaker and author, but I was brought to clear understanding of why I became these things. Your goal should be to ensure that people's lives can be better off because of what God has done in your life. God is the only One who can reveal the truth of yourself to you inside of your heart. It will begin only when you ask God to reveal that truth. When you learn the truth from God about who you are and why, you will be able to fulfill your purpose for living. It does not matter what your race may be, your religion, nor your circumstances. Once God reveals the truth to you, He will lead you through a course of obstacles that will test your character and ability to stay positive. After overcoming your obstacles, you will have realized what makes you truly unique and important. Afterwards, you will begin to not only believe in yourself, but you will love and admire yourself for exactly who God created you to be. You will no longer doubt yourself as a person, and, more importantly, you will no longer doubt God's ability to do good in your life. You will no longer be deceived into believing there are mistakes about you. This is because you will know yourself in accordance to how God created you and what He speaks in your heart.

Throughout your journey, you will encounter some changes in how others view you as a person, possibly even in your own family and best friends. As the Lord transforms you into a person of Him, you will be very much different from how you may have always been. It is going to be like a bright, shining light upon you that will be visible to all others. There will be those who will admire you greatly for who you have become, and there will be those who despise you heavily. Those who admire you will have most likely either found themselves in Jesus Christ or in the process of doing so. People who are trying every single day of their lives to do great and even better will find great inspiration in you and how you are conducting your life. By the contrary, those who will be hostile towards the person you have become will most likely have not found themselves in Jesus Christ and are not interested in doing so. They see all of the wonderful things in you they do not have, so they will insist on hating you to fill the void in their hearts. You may encounter some individuals seeking to bring you down and prevent you from fulfilling your divine purpose. People will talk about you negatively in secret, laugh at you, and regard you as crazy and inferior. You can overcome all of this through the strength of Jesus Christ, our Lord and Savior. All of the exact same things happened to Him. Jesus was beaten, spat upon, and regarded as crazy and inferior; however, He focused on His divine purpose, which was to rid the world from sin. Jesus did exactly that, and all of us are better off because of His sacrifices. Christ was the living proof that all of us can use to fulfill our purpose. It is His strength that will enable you to live the life that God has in store.

It will be important for you to ask the Lord to strengthen you along the many phases of your journey. It can become highly difficult and challenging to maintain a positive attitude. After learning of yourself and admiring the person you are, you will be able to love each and every other person of the world unconditionally. Because of where you have reached in your life, you are able to understand fully where others are and where they need to be. More importantly, you know how they can reach a new point in their lives that is based on the promises of God. This is what your life purpose is all about: perfecting the lives of individuals near and far. Every life that is transformed will lead to other lives for which will be transformed for the better. It will all begin with Jesus Christ. It will not work without Him, no matter how hard it is tried. Once you realize your divine gifts and find yourself in the Lord, you will be able to not only fulfill your purpose, but you will have peace and joy that no one without faith could ever understand.

I have endured the process of realizing the greatness of God within me. It began when I was sixteen years old and now I am nineteen. I know who I am in Jesus Christ and am able to live peacefully and stable in the midst of criticism and judgment. I continue to reach out to Jesus Christ for strength and wisdom everyday of the week.

I promised Him that I will never abandon His strength and disobey His fundamental commands. I promised Jesus that I would use all that He has given me to make the world a better place no matter what. I pray that you will reach out to the Lord Jesus to find yourself in Him and realize the things that make you unique. I pray also that you would turn away from leading a negative life based upon what others say or uncertain situations. I will pray that you are empowered to do great things on behalf of others and change lives for the better. You have the opportunity and ability for obtaining the tools and resources from Jesus Christ to make a difference in the world on behalf of God and His people. With God's help, you will be able to do exactly that. All you must do is ask Him to help you do so.

> And you shall know the Truth, and the Truth shall make you free. John 8:32

> To be wise you must have reverence for the Lord. If you know the Holy One, you will have understanding. Wisdom will and years to your life. You are the who will profit if you wisdom. If you reject it, you are the one who will suffer. Proverbs 9:10-12

> Jesus says, "I am the Resurrection. I am Life. Everyone who believes in me will have life even if they die." John 11:25

> And everyone who trusts in the Lord will be saved. Acts 2:21

> Jesus says, "If the world hates you, just remember that it has hated me first. If you belong to the world, then the world will have you as its own. But I chose you from this world, and you do not belong to it; that is why the world hates you." John 15:18

> Jesus says, "You did not choose me; I chose you. And I gave you this work: to go and produce fruit that will last. Then the Father will give you anything you ask for in my name. This is my command: Love each other. John 15:16

> You were told that your foolish desires will destroy you and that you must give up your old way of life with all its bad habits. Let the Spirit change your way of thinking and make you into a new person. You were created to be like God, and so must please Him and be truly holy. Ephesians 1:5-6

> If we can serve others, we should serve. If we can teach, we should teach. Romans 12:7

One and the Same Spirit gives faith to one person, while to another person He gives the power to heal. The Spirit gives one person the power to work miracles; to another, the gift of speaking God's message; and to yet another, the ability to tell the difference between gifts that come from the Spirit and those that do not. To one person He gives the ability to speak in strange tongues, and to another, He gives the ability to explain what is said. Corinthians 12:9-10

Do not copy the behavior and customs of this world, but let God transform you into a new person by changing the way you think. Then you will learn to know God's will for you, which is good and pleasing and perfect. Roman 12:2

Chapter 7

REAFFIRMING GOD'S MOST SACRED INSTITUTION

If you were to ever ask anyone, they would tell you most likely that the most difficult situations in the world to deal with are relationships and the issues that surround them. Pursuing a relationship with another person can add much stress and worry, along with other things to our daily lives. From personal experience, being in a relationship has always done more negative than positive. I can remember all of the different ways I have felt when I held feelings for certain girls. Besides the fact of being able to think only of particular girls that I was admiring at certain times, I felt more stressed than normal. I began eventually to feel depressed somewhat, especially if I was shot down with rejection. Before I entered my first relationship, I held this frustrating, cynical outlook pertaining relationships in general. I would say always that people should not involve themselves with relationships because they are only distractions and recipes for long-term destruction. From deep within, I desired to be joined with a beautiful, mature young lady to hold in my arms and share my life with. I desired this in the midst of a great skepticism about relationships and their outcomes. In the first chapter, you read all of the stories about the various encounters I have had with different girls; so I do not feel as if I must repeat them. I would proclaim, however, that all of the previous girls I developed interest in, except for one only, are not even close to my view of a legitimate, intellectual, and self-respected lady. It was not until after my first actual relationships had ended when my broad, cynical perspective on them began to change. I realized that it was wrong for me to cast off something for which is so complex and complicated before realizing it for myself truly. If Jesus Christ would have never came into my life and transformed my entire way of thinking and doing things, my outlook on not only relationships would have not matured, but on the world and life itself.

THE MOST SACRED INSTITUTION AMONG MAN

When God created in the beginning Adam and Eve, it was not only His intention but His solemn command for the both of them to be committed lovers and produce offspring. We must keep in mind that Adam and Eve were joined together and married by God Himself. If Eve would have never eaten from the Tree of good and evil, along with Adam to follow, the world would be very much different. There would be no sin, no evil, no pain, no tears from sorrow, no tragedy, and, certainly no need for war. One of the major sins, which spawned from Adam's and Eve's grave mistake, is that of sexual immorality. My intention is not to preach about morals and dictate to you that of which is in the Bible. Instead, I am seeking to encourage what is best in the long-term. All of us know that it says in the Bible that sex out of marriage, regardless of the circumstances, is wrong. It states also that marriage is strictly between a man and woman joined together by God as one. This is the reason that God has given to us all the ability to be attracted to those of the opposite sex.

As we have reached the ages of fourteen, fifteen, sixteen, and so on, the drive and desire for being intimate with some one of the opposite sex becomes a naturally driven element. As the days and months and years progress, the desire excels even greater. As the desires grows, our personality begins to transform, as does other things in our lives begin to change. With all of these different things happening to us, the fundamental priority in our hearts is to fulfill what our body desires heavily. All of the things we see with our eyes and hear with our ears just makes the entire situation worse off and exceedingly unbearable to deal with. But my question is very simple: what would be the best possible solution in the long-term? How would Jesus Christ want you to handle the situation so that He would be pleased?

God understands us all and our bodies better than we do. He wants to help us achieve what is in our hearts; as long as they do not involve sin, which is evil. The worst thing we could ever seek to accomplish is achieve what is in our hearts without the help of God. From personal experience, it is a grave struggle in pursuit of anything without reaching out to the One above for assistance. I realized with full, long-term trust in the Lord, all things are possible even if it may involve a prolonged, difficult battle. Dealing with testosterone can be a very difficult situation depending on who you are and your circumstances. We much too often receive visions of being intimate with a specific person or persons in general of the opposite sex, which does not help our situation by any measure. If we dwell in our minds on the things we do not have, our situation becomes much worse than normal. The worst thing for you to do is put yourself in a position where it becomes much more difficult for you to obey what God says. For example, you know God says for you to wait until you are married with the person He has in store to have sexual intercourse. If you are either alone with a particular male or female, or laying next to him or her, it will become impossible to resist having sexual intercourse. This may lead to an unintended pregnancy or even a sexually transmitted disease. Contraceptives will not exempt you from sin in the eyes of God. The best thing for you to do in the eyes of Him is not make any previsions, what-so-ever. It is you, the individual, who will be responsible for your situation.

All of the natural feelings, desires, and thoughts may encourage you to wish you were either in a committed relationship with a particular individual, or with as many of those of the opposite sex as you could handle. From a man's perspective, there has not been a single man who has walked the face of the Earth who has not wished that he could have it as easy as James Bond himself. All of us are nothing more than natural animals with a much higher level of thinking, which means that everyone gets aroused sexually and desires greatly to fulfill our natural desires. Because we as humans do have a much higher level of thinking and reasoning, we have a much better opportunity and greater sense of responsibility from God to do that of which He commands us. While we do have our natural desires, it does not give any of us the right to go against God's Word and do whatever we may want to do. We as humans have destroyed the foundation of God's institution of sex and marriage in an effort to seek pleasure and gain popularity. As we continue indulge in sexual sin and immorality, it leads us further and further away from God and His greatness. More importantly, it makes it even more difficult to achieve the desires He stored deep within our hearts. The task at hand is to revive God's most sacred institution of sex and marriage through faith and trust in Him for the long-term desires in our hearts.

Reclaiming the Greatness of God

The questions you must ask God are very simple: "what must I do to fulfill my natural desires? How can I go about doing this in a way that pleases you in the long-term? Could there be a possibility that you may have someone in store that I will spend the rest of my life with? If so, can you prepare me to the fullest extent for all that you have in store?" After you ask God these questions, put your life before your very self and examine who and where you are emotionally, mentally, and spiritually. As you examine the person you are, ask God to fix all of that for which that may be wrong inside and outside of yourself. Afterwards, ask God to help you find yourself and admire the person He created you to be. Ask God also to strengthen you by bringing you closer to Him and making you better person in His eyes. Once you know who you are truly and know what makes you happy in God's eyes, you will know exactly what to look for in a person that you may want to spend the rest of your life with.

There will always be those who will take advantage of others and use them for the sole purpose of fulfilling sexual gratification. These individuals do not know who they are and do not believe in themselves enough to treat others with dignity and respect. I encourage you to stay as far away from these type of individuals as you can because they serve as a fundamental threat to you and your faith in Jesus Christ as well as in yourself, and God does not want this for you. People like this will only break your heart and put a stain in your mind and heart about how relationships and marriage can and should be. The best thing to do is pray that God can transform the lives of these individuals and make them better persons in Him. God promises that if you obey and follow Him, He will reward you with the desires of your heart on His timing. He is the One who gave you the desires that you have, with the purpose of fulfilling the Will of God for your life. However, if you do not reach out the Lord and continue to do the same things you may have been doing for some time, nothing will change for the better.

From personal experience, I became much more joyful, stable, and optimistic when I refrained from associating with the particular girl who treated me terribly, while causing me a great deal of emotional pain and bondage. Life became so much greater when I put my primary focus on being the person who God created me to be, and I became as sure as ever that He has someone wonderful in store for the future. Every heartbreak, rejection, and betrayal was only a challenge from God to see whether or not you would begin serve and have faith in Him. It was to strengthen you in preparation for what He has planned in your future.

God has so many wonderful opportunities in store for you; however, He will not expose many of them to you until you are equipped fully to handle them. Also, things will not change for the better if you continue to do the same things that are keeping you where you are. God will not lead you forward if you disobey His word and refuse to reach out to Him in prayer and thanksgiving. There is absolutely no justification in disobeying God and His commands. Pray to God to strengthen you in times of great difficulty. If you reach out to Him in patience and humility, He will not only unite you with the person He has in store, but you will experience the full extent of God's profound greatness in your life and those in your presence.

> Avoid immorality. Any other sin a man commits does not affect his body; but the man who is guilty of sexual immorality sins against his own body. 1 Corinthians 6:18

> Have respect for marriage. Always be faithful to your partner, because God will punish anyone who is immoral or unfaithful in marriage. Hebrews 13:4

> Nevertheless, because of sexual immorality, let each man have his own wife, and let each woman have her husband. 1 Corinthians 7:2

> Jesus says, "If any man will come after Me, let him deny himself, and take up his cross daily, and follow Me. For whosoever will save his life shall lose it; but whosoever will lose his life for My sake, the same shall save it." Luke 9:23-24

Chapter 8

DESTINY IS CALLING YOUR SUCCESS

As a firm believer in the values of faith, hard work, and education, I am deeply privileged and honored to stand before each of you today. It is always in great pleasure for me to stand before people like you in an effort to inspire a new generation of individuals to achieve greatness for the future. I was born in Chicago, IL. I am currently a senior at one of the best and finest high-schools in the entire nation. After high-school, I plan to attend a top university and earn a PhD in political science, a Bachelor's Degree in speech, and a Juris Doctor in criminal law. After college, I aspire to become a high-school teacher of government and history, then a college professor of political science, and then I will pursue a career in politics. My first published book, *The Advancement of Common Humanity*, advocates a renewed sense of unity and patriotism in American politics. My second book, *The Call of Destiny: A Liberation from Apathy, Shame, and Failure*, calls for a return to the values of hard work, strong character, and individual initiative. Most importantly, I advocate the profound importance for each individual to get the best education and lead a career of successful achievement.

As many of you can see, I aspire deep within myself to be the best at everything I participate within. When I was much younger, never for once did I think that I would be the person standing here today. I can remember always aspiring to be someone great. I aspired always to be a person that people admired greatly. There soon came a time when this would begin to become possible. It all began five years ago on July 11th, 2006 when my family moved from Chicago, IL to a small, rural community in central Louisiana. In the beginning, it was the worst experience of my entire life. I had no real friends, I knew absolutely no person, and I was bullied everyday at school. All I could do was feel shameful and depressed, but there was always hope. I became an honor roll student and excelled academically. And then on March 1st, 2008 my life would change forever when I accepted Jesus Christ as my Life, Lord, and Savior.

I became interested strongly in politics and public speaking, and on September 2nd, 2009 my first book, *The Advancement of Common Humanity*, was published. For two consecutive years, I won 1st place Superior at the District Speech Rally, and 2nd at State, and I was the first person ever from my school to do so. In July of 2010, I began and completed my second book, and on February 10th, 2011, *The Call of Destiny* was published. I have spoken at many schools, churches, and local events, emphasizing the profound importance in hard work and self-determination. Today, I aspire to be a successful lawyer, teacher, professor, and some day the President of the United States of America. It will always be a fundamental obligation for me to lead a future of great fortune, limitless prosperity, and successful achievement.

So as all of you can see, I am most likely to lead a very successful career. Nothing, besides my devout Christian faith, is more important in my life than that. The reason I am here today is to inspire each and everyone of you to realize the greatness within yourself and unleash your full potential to be as successful as you can be in your life and career. How many of you can define the meaning of real success? My vision of success is very simple: it is reading and studying and writing to get the best education that will provide the best jobs and occupations to support yourselves. It means living the best lives in our teenage years so that ten, fifteen, and twenty years from today we can educate and inspire our children to achieve the things in their hearts. Each of us should aspire to become lawyers and doctors and professors and CEOs. For we know that real success is accompanied always by the best education. I believe profoundly in the ability of each and every young person to obtain a college education because real success is less likely to be achieved without it. In the words of Malcolm X, "Education is our passport to the future; for the future belongs to those who prepare for it today." Now is the time for each of us to realize our full potential and ambition to lead the best, most successful future upon our capacity. To truly be as successful as we can be, each of us as individuals must believe in ourselves, assume full responsibility for achieving our goals, and work as hard as we can to get the job done.

As each of us prepare to fully unleash our potential, the most important thing we must do is believe in the person of whom God created us to be. As God created each of us in His image, He stored within each of us certain talents and abilities and the potential to achieve greatness in our lives. Each and everyone of us has greatness stored deep within us; greatness of which can be used to advance not only ourselves but others as well. However, it is up to you to believe in yourself and strive to achieve the things you want. You are obligated to envision a future of prosperity and success for yourself, and do what needs to be done to transform your hopes and dreams into reality such as reading books and working hard in school. Never believe for one second of your journey that you are somewhat limited to a certain degree of achievement or doomed to an inevitable fate. No matter where you come from and no matter what the situation may consist of, you can do anything you put your mind to. You can become a lawyer, a doctor, a CEO, a law enforcer, or the President of the United States of America. You could even become a famous athlete or actor or celebrity. You can get the best education, pursue a successful career, live in a nice house and raise a loving, caring family.

How many of you watch VH1 and MTV? Sometimes the famous singers and celebrities show off their homes and cars. As you are watching this on TV, I bet you are thinking to yourself, "Wow! That is a really big house and a nice car. I wish I could have that." My advice to each one of you is to never wish for greatness in your life, but know deep within your heart that you have the exact same opportunity as everyone else have to achieve wealth and luxury. When life gets hard, you should pray to Christ for the wisdom, knowledge, and strength to advance in your journey. There is no doubt that there will be times in our lives when we struggle and fail, but the true strength of your character is determined on whether or not you rise above the struggle and excel stronger and better than ever before. You will not win every contest, you will defeat every battle, and you will definitely not be accepted by everyone. This is true for me, it was true for all the greatest people that each of us admire, and it will definitely be the case throughout the course of your life and career. I believe, however, in each of you to advance from every struggle, realize the greatness within you, and unleash that greatness upon the world.

As we empower our ability to be successful, we must also take full responsibility for doing the things we must do to get ahead. While it is the responsibility of our parents and teachers and close friends to encourage us to lead the best possible lives, no one else is responsible for fulfilling your obligations to succeed in your career. You are the one who is responsible for reading and studying and going to the library and getting the best education. You are obligated to set high expectations for a successful career and motivate yourself to do great things such as writing books and going to the best college. In this country you write your own destiny and you decide what kind of future you will lead based on the decisions and choices you make today. Each and everyone of us has the opportunity and ability to lead the most successful and satisfying career possible. It is with each one of us to use this opportunity to the best of ourselves. If you become successfully wealthy or financially stable, it is because you worked hard and sacrificed and persevered yourself to the fullest. If you become poor or less fortunate, it is most likely because you did not make the best decisions or you did not work hard enough and obtain the best education. The only person who can limit how much you can achieve is you. Your race, your skin color, your family, and your background does not determine how much you can achieve, but instead whether or not you choose to do the things to excel such as learning and praying and getting an education. So let us prepare to exemplify our strength to achieve our full potential.

As we assume responsibility for doing what needs to be done, so must we work as hard as we can in our career. Hard work is the most fundamental ideal of successful achievement. All of us here today have certain skills and imaginations within ourselves. Some of us seek to become famous singers or actors, or in my example, a successful politician. None of these things will ever come about through the blink of an eye. If you truly seek to fulfill the dreams within you, you should ask God to give you the patience and guidance to lead in your journey. Each of our desires and talents and abilities are not the same as others. Some of us are athletic, while many of us are verbal and white-collar. I strongly believe that every teenager upon graduation should go to college because most of the high-salary occupations such as lawyers and doctors and professors require four or more years of higher education, but if there is something that you desire greatly and it does not require much or any college, then do what is best for you. Just know deep within yourself that it can be you who create the next iPod or iPad or iPhone. It can be you who develop the next computer brand or car brand or game system. On this day, let us get involved in school activities and unleash our ambitions to lead the best career possible upon our capacity.

As we view the larger world around us, we would learn that things are not great as they could be. The future of the world in which you and I live depends upon the work we do today. If each of us can get the best education and achieve wealth and success, our children in future years can inherit a society of hope, opportunity, and greatness. In my own life, I aspire deeply to lead and inspire a new generation of Americans and people of the world into the future; a future where dreams are possible and hope is alive and success can become a reality for all of those who believe and strive. This is the world I envision. A world where ordinary people can do extraordinary things. There are no such things as poor people or rich people or middle-class people, but instead people who can defy the odds and lead lives of peace, luxury, and harmony. Each and everyone of you can achieve greatness and wealth and fortune for yourself and your family and so on; for this should be the greatest aspiration for each of us to accomplish.

Success is never a given, but instead a moral responsibility of every man and woman once he or she is brought into the world. I ask you to begin the journey of setting and meeting your goals to become the person who will not only do the things that are necessary, but things that are unspeakable and unimaginable such as writing books and building large businesses and becoming the President of the United States. Each of us should aspire to be the greatest individuals that will ever live, people that the world will admire for centuries to come, and we should be those who made the world a better place for generations to come. Life should mean so much more than just being a normal and ordinary person; for it should be your top priority to lead the best and most successful life that you can. If an African-American from inner-city Chicago can write and publish two books at the age of seventeen, write and present speeches, and aspire someday to become the second African-American President of the United States, then each of you can realize your full potential to do all the things that you wish. At this moment, I ask for all of you to never give up on your dreams, get the best education, make a difference on behalf of the future, and change the world. On this day, let us pledge once more to answer the call of destiny: successful achievement on every journey we shall pursue. Let it be us!

Thank you! God Bless you! And may God Bless the United States of America!

Destiny is

Calling Your

Success

Chapter 9

SCRIPTURES AND QUOTES

Isaiah 58:11 "The LORD will guide you continually, And satisfy your soul in drought, And strengthen your bones; You shall be like a watered garden, And like a spring of water, whose waters do not fail."

Be prepared. You're up against far more than you can handle on your own. Take all the help you can get, every weapon God has issued, so that when it's all over but the shouting you'll still be on your feet. Truth, righteousness, peace, faith, and salvation are more than words. Learn how to apply them. You'll need them throughout your life. God's Word is an indispensable weapon. In the same way, prayer is essential in this ongoing warfare. Pray hard and long. Pray for your brothers and sisters. Keep your eyes open. Keep each other's spirits up so that no one falls behind or drops out. Ephesians 6:13-18

James 1:22-24 "But be doers of the word, and not hearers only, deceiving yourselves. For if anyone is a hearer of the word and not a doer, he is like a man observing his natural face in a mirror; for he observes himself, goes away, and immediately forgets what kind of man he was."

2 Corinthians 10:5 We demolish arguments and every pretension that sets itself up against the knowledge of God, and we take captive every thought to make it obedient to Christ.

Isaiah 53:7 "He was treated harshly, but endured it humbly; he never said a word. Like a lamb about to be slaughtered, like a sheep about to be sheared, he never said a word. Matthew 27:11-14 Jesus stood before the

Roman governor, who questioned him. "Are you the king of the Jews?" he asked. "So you say," answered Jesus. But he said nothing in response to the accusations of the chief priests and elders. So Pilate said to him, "Don't you hear all these things they accuse you of?" But Jesus refused to answer a single word, with the result that the Governor was greatly surprised.

"No weapon formed against you shall prosper, and every tongue that rises against you in judgment you shall condemn; this is the heritage of the servants of the Lord." Isaiah 54-17

Live a life filled with love, following the example of Christ. He loved us and offered himself as a sacrifice for us, a pleasing aroma to God. (Ephesians 5:2)

Whoever pursues righteousness and unfailing love will find life, righteousness, and honor. (Proverbs 21:21)

Beloved, let us love one another, for love is from God; and everyone who loves is born of God and knows God. 1 John 4:7

"Have faith in God. What I'm about to tell you is true. Suppose one of you says to this mountain, 'Go and throw yourself into the sea.' You must not doubt in your heart. You must believe that what you say will happen. Then it will be done for you. So I tell you, when you pray for something, believe that you have already received it. Then it will be yours. And when you stand praying, forgive anyone you have anything against. Then your Father in Heaven will forgive your sins."—From Matthew 11:22-26 (NIRV)

The Spirit produces love, joy, peace, patience, kindness, goodness, faithfulness, humility, and self-control. There is no law against such things as these. Galatians 5:22-23

Have I not commanded you? Be strong and of good courage; do not be afraid, nor be dismayed, for the Lord your God is with you wherever you go. (Joshua 1:9)

Remember to show your brother love . . . only love . . . .
"For our struggle is not against flesh and blood, but against the rulers, against the authorities, against the powers of this dark world and against the spiritual forces of evil in the heavenly realms."~ Ephesians 6:12

He gave Himself for us, that He might redeem us from every lawless deed and purify for Himself His own special people, zealous for good works. Titus 2:14

Revelation 1:17-18 "17 When I saw him, I fell at his feet as though dead. But he laid his right hand on me, saying, "Fear not, I am the first and the last, 18. and the living one. I died, and behold I am alive forevermore, and I have the keys of Death and Hades." JESUS SPEAKS: "Father, I want those you have given me to be with me where I am, and to see my glory, the glory you have given me because you loved me before the creation of the world." John 17:24

"Therefore if you have been raised up with Christ, keep seeking the things above, where Christ is, seated at the right hand of God.Set your mind on the things above, not on the things that are on earth.For you have died and your life is hidden with Christ in God." ~Colossians 3:1-3

There is no fear in love; but perfect love casteth out fear.—1 John 4:8

Ecclesiastes 5:2-5 Think before you speak, and don't make any rash promises to God. He is in heaven and you are on earth, so don't say any more than you have to. The more you worry, the more likely you are to have bad dreams, and the more you talk, the more likely you are to say something foolish. So when you make a promise to God, keep it as quickly as possible. He has no use for a fool. Do what you promise to do. Better not to promise at all than to make a promise and not keep it.

Matthew 18:19 Again I say unto you, That if two of you shall agree on earth as touching any thing that they shall ask, it shall be done for them of my Father which is in Heaven.

But I will bless the person who puts his trust in me. He is like a tree growing near a stream and sending out roots to the water. It is not afraid when hot weather comes, because its leaves stay green; it has no worries when there is no rain; it keeps on bearing fruit.—Jeremiah 17:7-8 (GNT)

Verily, verily, I say unto you, He that heareth my word, and believeth on him that sent me, hath everlasting life, and shall not come into condemnation; but is passed from death unto life. John 5:24

Ask, and it shall be given you; seek, and ye shall find; knock, and it shall be opened unto you: For every one that asketh receiveth; and he that seeketh findeth; and to him that knocketh it shall be opened. Matt 7:7-8

Proverbs 3:5-7 Trust in the Lord with all your heart. Never rely on what you think you know. Remember the Lord in everything you do, and he will show you the right way. Never let yourself think that you are wiser than you are; simply obey the Lord and refuse to do wrong.

Always be joyful and never stop praying. Whatever happens, keep thanking God because of Jesus Christ. This is what God wants you to do.—1 Thessalonians 5:16-18

Jesus says, "Behold, I send you out as sheep in the midst of wolves. There be wise as serpents and harmless as doves. But beware of men, for they will deliver you up to councils and scourge you in their synagogues. You will be brought before governors and kings for My sake, as a testimony to them and for the Gentiles. But they will deliver you up, do not worry about how or what you should speak. For it will be given to you in that hour what you should speak; for it is not you who speak, but the Spirit of your Father who speaks in you." Matthew 10:16-20

With the strength of God You can do and endure and overcome all things. God is the source of your endurance and the Power of your might. There is nothing gained or received in your life worth more than the friendship of God.. (John15:15). I no longer call you servants, because a servant does not know His master's business. Instead, I have called you friends.

"I give them eternal life, and they shall never perish; no one will snatch them out of my hand. My Father, who has given them to me, is greater than all no one can snatch them out of my Father's hand." ~ John 10:28-29

"Don't copy the behavior and customs of this world, but let God transform you into a new person by changing the way you think. Then you will learn to know God's will for you, which is good and pleasing and perfect."—Romans 12:2

One and the same Spirit gives faith to one person, while to another person he gives the power to heal. The Spirit gives one person the power to work miracles; to another, the gift of speaking God's message; and to yet another, the ability to tell the difference between gifts that come from the Spirit and those that do not. To one person he gives the ability to speak in strange tongues, and to another he gives the ability to explain what is said.—Corinthians 12:9-10

God is our shelter and strength, always ready to help in times of trouble. So we will not be afraid, even if the earth is shaken and mountains fall into the ocean depths; even if the seas roar and rage, and the hills are shaken by the violence.—Psalm 46:1-3

Don't worry about anything, but pray about everything. With thankful hearts offer up your prayers and requests to God. Then, because you belong to Christ Jesus, God will bless you with peace that no one can completely understand. And this peace will control the way you think and feel.—Philippians 4:6-7

If we can serve others, we should serve. If we can teach, we should teach.—Romans 12:7

"You know about Jesus of Nazareth and how God poured out on him the Holy Spirit and power. He went everywhere, doing good and healing all who were under the power of the Devil, for God was with him. We are witnesses of everything that he did in the land of Israel and in Jerusalem. Then they put him to death by nailing him to a cross. But God raised him from death three days later and caused him to appear, not to everyone, but only to the witnesses that God had already chosen, that is, to us who ate and drank with him after he rose from death. And he commanded us to preach the gospel to the people and to testify that he is the one whom God has appointed judge of the living and the dead. All the prophets spoke about him, saying that all who believe in him will have their sins forgiven through the power of his name." (Acts 10:38-43)

No discipline is enjoyable while it is happening—it's painful! But afterward there will be a peaceful harvest of right living for those who are trained in this way. (Hebrews 12:11)

The Lord will maintain the cause of the afflicted, and execute justice for the needy. Psalm 140:12

You are a personal representative of Jesus, so put on behavior that is going to represent Him. (Col. 3:12)

2 Corinthians 4:17 And this small and temporary trouble we suffer will bring us a tremendous and eternal glory, much greater than the trouble. 18

For we fix our attention, not on things that are seen, but on things that are unseen. What can be seen lasts only for a time, but what cannot be seen lasts forever.

For our struggle is not against flesh and blood, but against the rulers, against the authorities, against the powers of this dark world and against the spiritual forces of evil in the heavenly realms. Ephesians 6:12

John 3:16 "For God So Loved the World That He Gave His Only Begotten Son, and for those who believe in and worship Him (Jesus Christ) shall not perish but will have eternal life."

"I learned that courage was not the absence of fear, but the triumph over it. The brave man is not he who does not feel afraid, but he who conquers that fear."

—Nelson Mandela

"Choosing to be positive and having a grateful attitude is going to determine how you're going to live your life."

—Joel Osteen

"If there is no struggle, there is no progress. Those who profess to favor freedom, and yet deprecate agitation, are men who want crops without plowing up the ground, they want rain without thunder and lightning. They want the ocean without the awful roar of its many waters."

—Frederick Douglass

Acknowledgements

I am grateful eternally and in the name of God to be the person that I am today. I am proud deeply of my accomplishments and how far I have traveled on this journey. It took a great deal of faith and determination in overcoming so many obstacles and achieve many of the things God has in store. As I reminisce on how far I have come, I realize that I would not have been successful if it were not for the many who have helped me along the way. There have been so many others who have acted on my behalf. They have served not only as friends, but have sacrificed heavily for me on so many occasions. Many of them have advised and assisted me spiritually, and helped lift me when I was down. I acknowledge with all of my heart that God is the One who has preordained for these individuals to be in my life at certain times for specific outcomes to be produced. God uses people to fulfill His works and accomplish miracles on Earth. God, as well as many people in my life, has bestowed upon me the benefit of the doubt in so many instances, and I do not know where I would be otherwise. I am going to acknowledge many of those who have played a fundamental role in helping me become the person I am today. I will acknowledge also a number of individuals who I admire heavily. The order in which each person or party is mentioned is strictly indifferent to how much he or she means to me; for each of them hold a special place in my heart and soul.

First and foremost, I would like to acknowledge my Life, Lord and Savior, Jesus Christ. My relationship with Him is definitely one of the greatest things that I could ever be grateful for. The love and feelings I have for Jesus are unexplainable and, most importantly, uncompromising in all circumstances. I admire the Lord for not only clearing my way into Heaven, but for revealing to me how to live a great and wonderful life. I love Him also for the luxurious, abundant future He has in store, while strengthening me each and every day to fulfill His commands. In every struggle, crisis, and injustice, Jesus has led me forward and ensured that I was as wise and strong as ever before. There has been times when I had become very angry and upset. Instead of dwelling upon those feelings and boasting in negativity, which is not what Christ wants, I resorted to His strength as my feelings would be resolved fully by Him. Because of Jesus Christ, I am lonely never, discouraged rarely, and motivated always to help people. Everything that can be considered mine by others, from my perspective, belongs actually to Jesus Christ. All things that would be considered unfair will be repaid with wonderful blessings from Him. Jesus and I have shared many moments, as we will share much longer and greater ones as this journey progresses. I will never abandon my lasting commitment to God, as He has promised to never abandon me. From this day and beyond eternity, I will always love my Heavenly Father, the Lord God Jesus Christ with each and every piece of my entire heart.

In every great person's life, he or she must always take great joy in who he or she was created to be. However, he or she is absolutely nothing without family. I could never be more grateful in the name of God for the two individuals that I know as my mother and father, Dawn Johnson and Nathan Augustine, respectively. I remember all the times they have been there for me and cared for me no matter what. They nurtured me when I was sick, rescued me when I experienced trouble, and supported me when I was in need. There were many instances in the past for which I was bullied at school. In many of these instances, they went to the school and demanded that the situation be brought to a halt. I will always remember the rides on the L Train, the family car, the walks to and from school and the grocery store, the laughs, the cries, and the hugs and kisses. I will remember every single moment I have shared with my mom and dad. I would certainly not be the person I am and have many of the things I need and want if it were not for them. Their love for me was shown during the times I would wake up in the middle of the night as a little kid crying from a terrible nightmare. Their love was shown as I was successful in many things, as well as in times when I was not very successful. In every earnest effort, I could never be able to express the fullness of the love and admiration I share for my mother and father. For as long as I have breath in each of my two lungs, I will be truly grateful for every bit of love I have received from my parents. All of that which was given to me from them will be passed onto my children and grandchildren in the future. I also love my four older brothers, Nathaniel, Steven, Jerome, and Jermaine with all of my heart. They have always been there for me no matter what. I love all of my aunties, uncles, and cousins very much. I love also every in-law with all of my heart. I will always be grateful eternally for the family that God has conceived me into, and I will never, ever forget who and where I have come from.

As I advance on this journey, I believe with all of my heart that I would not be the person I am if I had not attended Avoyelles High School. Avoyelles High School has played a fundamental role in molding important aspects of my character and my broad view of the world. One of the best things I love about my old school is that teachers are willing to talk about more than just academics. If I felt ever the need to talk about something important, I felt very comfortable in doing so. I have certainly shared a good number ups and downs at Avoyelles High, but they have always strengthened me along the way. The event that led to my spiritual uprising in

2010 would not have taken place if I did not attend AHS. I enjoyed every class, club, activity, and field trip while attending AHS. I am definitely grateful for all of the lasting friendships that were created, and also for all of those at the school who regard we with great respect and high admiration. There are those who feel as if Avoyelles High is not a great school. People can proclaim all that they please about this school, but my story alone proves something that is totally different. I will always consider AHS my home as well as my school at heart, and I will always love, admire, pray for, and support Avoyelles High School. Some special friends of mine from Avoyelles High include Daderinne Denae Thibodeaux, Hannah Desselle, Mya Bordelon, Larry Martin, Samantha Maxwell, Austin Davis, Austin Johnson, Emily Bass, Regis Perry, Abigail Clark (and her baby), Terra Wilson, Tevin Wilson, Kevin Polk, Marlee Ducote, Tessa Nicole, Lindsey Tyler, Emily Sherman, Emily Longino, Clarence Dibble, Lena Lemoine, Gavyn Chesne, Kirkland Greene, Robert Shallington, Autumn Johnson, Ali Riche, Humneet Sandhu, Summer Sandhu, Jade Alexis, Stacy Maria, Christopher McKay, Ian Turner, Kandace St. Romain, Diana St. Romain, Aric Gulliver, Chelsea Rabalais, Jessica Hess, Travon Wright, Heidi Lemoine Hernandez, Steven Hernandez, Sabrina Roberts, Madison Rogers, Christina Ann Olexy, Malcolm Hagger, Abigail Wilson, Melissa Messer, Michelle Messer, Courtney Lynn Bordelon, Nicholas Grindstaff, Kevin Dupont, Brittany Moore, Chelsea Tippit, Nathan Tippit, Rachael Martin, Payton Miller, Hannah Bordelon, Charles Charrier, Ernest Charrier, Benjamin Wellman, Bryan Dawson, Omar Dawson, Kelsey Osman, Twanna Tyler, Shauntel Puckett, Sonya Durand, Eugenia Desselle, Ashley Smith, Sophia Roy, Brandon Legnion, Matthew Murdock, Dan Soldani, Scott Balius, and so many more!

While being a student at Avoyelles High, I became acquainted greatly with my content mastery instructor, Mr. Joel Tassin. I still remember vividly the very first day he called me into his classroom (P-16) to discuss the services offered in content mastery. The date of this was August 18, 2008. The relationship that he and I shared was unique by a great measure. As one of his students, he always did his profound best while assisting me in my studies. Our student-teacher relationship soon phased into one of the greatest friendships I could have ever asked for. Mr. Joel served as a mentor and helper to me. If I had ever any questions or concerns about anything, Mr. Joel would be there to fill me in. He was there when I would have issues with other students, as well as with other school-related issues. If I were ever doing something that he considered counterproductive in the long-term, he would advise me strongly of what is right and hold me responsible for my decisions. I will never forget the day he showed me a great way to read the Holy Bible when he saw me reading it. The date of this was April 13, 2012. One of my favorite things in the world was our frequent discussions about political matters, which was more fun to me than educational. There has been various situations where I would have been compromised heavily if it were not for the extended help of Mr. Joel. The thing that makes me the most glad about working with him is knowing that he wanted nothing but the best for me in the long-term. He is a wonderful person as well as a great teacher. Even while I am no longer a student in high-school, Mr. Joel will be recognized in my life always with high regards. I will always admire and respect Mr. Joel Tassin not only as my former teacher, but as my friend and mentor. I pray that God will continue to bless him and use him for the betterment of others.

Along the friendship of Mr. Joel Tassin, I admire my high-school principal, Mr. Brent Whiddon, with all of that for which I have. I could think never of anyone else I would have liked to serve as my principal during this time in my life. Avoyelles High School could have never asked for a greater man to be it's principal. There has been times when Mr. Brent would stay overnight at the school for certain things that needed to be done on behalf of the school and the students. I enjoyed greatly assisting him in helping Avoyelles High continue to be the great school for which it is. Every morning when I came to school I would greet him with a handshake. He would greet me during the afternoons at lunch and before school ended for the day. He would assist me if I ever needed rides to and from school-related functions. Mr. Brent served also as a mentor to me in many ways, which helped me become a much greater person over the years. I remember becoming agitated somewhat during my senior year because none of my teachers would nominate me for student-of-the-month. It was Mr. Brent who nominated me for the last month in which a student could be nominated. He rewarded me with the Principal's Cup at the annual award's ceremony. I will always consider him a great friend and my school principal deep within my heart. I look forward humbly to the lunch that the both of us have planned upon my graduation from law school. I will always appreciate all that Mr. Brent has done for me and on behalf of Avoyelles High School, and I pray that the greatness of God continues to reign superior in his life. I pray also that God continues to strengthen him to be the great principal that he has always been. I am fully grateful also for all the vice-principals who served during the time I was at Avoyelles High School: Ms. Jennifer Dismer, Ms. Theresa Despino, Ms. Mary Speer, and Ms. Roxana Butler.

One of the greatest relationships that I am most grateful for is the one I have with Mrs. Kathy Lemoine. I have known her always, however, as Ms. KK. I can say on everything that I have that Ms. KK is one of the best teachers in the entire world. She is also one of the best friends and mentors I could ever ask for. I remember the very first day that I ever heard her speak. It was instructing me to remove my hat inside the school building. We began to become acquainted better as I was preparing to compete for the very first time in the district speech rally. It was this particular experience that led Ms. KK and I to become very close. Everyday when school was dismissed I would go peak my head inside her class and tell her to have a nice day. The following year was when she became my speech teacher, along with English during the two years after. During my sophomore year, we would eat lunch together everyday at school. We would have detailed discussions about politics, religion, etc.

We would always have conversations about important things that pertained to life in general. I could always rely on Ms. KK for anything I needed help with. I still remember the day that she came to my house to tell me that I had won first place in the district speech rally, which was the very day that Jesus Christ began to change my life forever. The date of this day was April 5, 2010. Ms. KK has assisted me on a great number of occasions, and I appreciate highly everything she has done on my behalf. She has helped me become a better speaker over time, and she deserves much credit for my great success at the district and state rallies. I will never forget any of the things Ms. KK has done for me when I reach God's final destination. I will always love and respect her no matter where I am in my life. I will pray that our connection not only ends never, but grows continuously beyond eternity.

During my junior year at Avoyelles High School, I became very good friends with one of the Jr. high teachers, Mr. Scotty P. Dauzat. I consider Scotty one of the best friends I have, as well as a brother-in-Christ. He is one of the strongest, most loyal Christians that I know. The first time I remember seeing Scotty was during an assembly at school in the gymnasium, but we did not exchange words. It was during school in December of 2010 that I was walking to my next class when he and I first communicated and became the best of friends. He asked me simply how my day was going, and I told him with a smile on my face that it was going as great as ever. He asked me afterwards if I was a believer in Jesus Christ, and I told him absolutely. The both of us began to attend church together sometimes, which I enjoyed heavily. We would have breakfast and lunch together at various times. If I need ever any questions answered or concerns to be met, Scotty does his best always to assist me in however he could. The best part about the friendship between Scotty and myself is that we can trust each other with what we tell one another. I can trust in God that he will always help guide me in the right direction. Scotty was there for me always when I needed support, and I have great faith that he will continue to do so. I am grateful eternally for our friendship and for all of the things he has done on my behalf. I will continue to pray for God's blessing upon the life of Scotty P. Dauzat as well as the lives of his children and their mom.

After speaking at an event in honor of the birthday of Dr. Martin Luther King, Jr., I met a wonderful man named Damon Didier and his wife Danielle. The both of them are two of the nicest individuals that I have ever met in my entire life. At the time when I first met Damon, he was a candidate for sheriff here in our local area. I did not see him again until seven months after. I had forgotten his name, but I remembered meeting him and his wife vividly. It was at a football jamboree where I finally saw him again as he was campaigning for sheriff. We talked for about a genuine fifteen minutes as we caught up after seven months. He told me that the speech that I gave at the MLK event was one of the best speeches he heard ever. He told me also that a large number of people have yet to forget the words that I have spoken. There would be more opportunities for the both of us to become acquainted better and grow our friendship to what it is today. I can proclaim honestly that Damon Didier is one of the greatest persons I know, and I am very glad to have him as a friend. He has inspired me with his resolve, as well as his commitment to his wife and children. It was such a great honor to stand by him in his campaign for sheriff, and I wish still to this very day that he was elected. Damon and I have had many interesting conversations ranging from faith in God to political matters to faith in God. He has assisted me on various occasions, which I appreciate greatly. I appreciate also the birthday cake that he delivered to my house by surprise. I would like also to thank Damon's wife, Danielle, for being there when needed. I will continue to pray that their children's future is wonderful and great in the name of Jesus Christ. I look forward humbly to seeing Damon Didier and his wife when he returns home in just a couple of months. I have great faith that God has something spectacular in store for him politically, and I pray that he will run again for sheriff in the future and get elected to office.

During the summer of 2012, I became great friends with a minister named Rosa Pierite. She and I worked together on a summer program known as Soldiers in Christ for children throughout the area. I was one of the instructors for the program, and we would alternate talking to the different groups. I believe with all of my heart that she was a blessing from God in my life. It was Minister Pierite who assisted me heavily during the time I was distressed emotionally due to my relationship troubles. All of the support and wisdom she had to offer helped me open my eyes to many things that I had never known. I remember the day when she told me that I should save all of that for which I have to offer for my wife in the future. She told me also that I should associate myself with people who are strong in Jesus Christ so that His strength could rub off onto me. The date of this June 26, 2012. She told me also to think about how my walk in Christ would be affected if I tried to rebuild my relationship with a previous girlfriend. Everything she told me made perfect sense, and she helped me realize there are lots of people who would not have assisted me in the ways that she did. After recovering from all of that for which I was experiencing, all of that for which she advised me became as clear as it did before. I praise Jesus Christ heavily for putting her in my life to help me revive. To the current day, Minister Rosa and I are still very close friends, and if I ever need assistance for things she helps me the best way she could. I will continue to pray that she and her entire family remain strong positively in the Lord Jesus Christ as they live in peace and hope for the future.

During the year 2011, I met a man named Wilbert Holland at a church near my house. Wilbert is a very strong person in Jesus Christ, and he is a very helpful, dependable individual. He and I have attended church together, fellowshipped with one another, and enjoyed many pleasant conversations. Wilbert offered a great deal of spiritual assistance when I experiencing hardship during the Summer of 2012. I will always be grateful for all of the things he has done on my behalf. I will pray that God continues to bless Wilbert Holland with His greatness, and strengthen him each and every day of his life.

On the very last day of June in the year 2012, I met a man named Marshall Pierite. Mr. Pierite became aware of me through one of his sisters. I was telling her about the books I had written and published and that I am a motivational speaker. She was impressed greatly and had taken down my contact information. She told me then about her brother Marshall Pierite and the work he does. A few days later I received a phone call from Mr. Pierite asking if the both of us could get together and talk. He and I met a few days later and got to know each other somewhat. I was very impressed by how strong Mr. Pierite is in Jesus Christ, and he had a great deal of wisdom to offer. He told me that I would be able to come with him to South Dakota for a Christian youth rally that was being held. I was offered a speaking role, and received the opportunity to meet a famous Christian rap star, E. Daniel, who was performing there. I also became acquainted with Mr. Pierite's wife and daughter, who were in attendance during the trip. This trip to South Dakota was the most important thing that happened for me in very long time. It was what God used to revive me from all that I was experiencing during the summer of 2012. I consider all of them a major part of my life, I am best friends with each of them, and I love them with every piece of my heart and soul. I pray that God continues to bless them with so many wonderful things, and that all of us can continue being very close to one another.

During the height of my eighth grade school year, I was assigned to a speech therapist named Jeanie Akridge. In the beginning, I was shy somewhat of working with her. As time went on, however, I began to benefit from and enjoy working with her on my speech. There came a time when we can began to discuss spiritual matters and read from scripture, and this is what spawned our wonderful friendship. Through Jeanie, I met her husband Frank Akridge. At the time, he was a pastor at a church that I would go to sometimes. On many occasions, the three of us would attend church and have lunch afterwards. I have considered Frank and Jeanie two very special and important people in my life for over a few years now. They have assisted me a great number of times, and they have always been there if I was ever down. I have learned many important things from the both of them about faith in God, political matters, and life concerns in general. There were times when much of their advice would seem unclear, but I would learn always later on of the many things they tried to teach me. I would never be able to fully thank God for the great friendship that I share with Frank and Jeanie, and I will always appreciate everything they have done on my behalf. I pray that they will always continue to serve Jesus Christ and be the wonderful individuals they are.

While being a freshman at Avoyelles High School, I became great friends with my then-speech therapist, Lillie Armand. I can proclaim honestly that she is one of the greatest persons that I have ever met in my life. She had much great advice to offer me for many things that were of concern to me. When I began to work on a speech for a competition, she assisted me in making it one of the greatest speeches that I have ever written. We would discuss issues concerning politics, faith in Jesus Christ, and other related issues. All of the things we worked on in speech therapy helped me not only improve my speech, but it helped me become a better person for the future. The following year, she said that I improved so much that I no longer needed speech therapy. I really did begin to miss meeting with her once a week and having our discussions. I was always a person who heavily enjoyed talking with people about many things. It always helped me realize how important and great life really is, and working with Ms. Lillie Armand certainly did just that. I will always be grateful in the name of God for all that was done for me by her. I hope that there will come a time when I will have the opportunity to repay her for how much my life improved because of Ms. Lillie Armand.

While being a student at Mansura Middle School, I became acquainted greatly with my then-principal, Mr. Allen Warnersdorfer. On the current day, I consider Mr. Allen a very special friend and important individual in my life. He knew always of all the things I am capable of accomplishing. I remember the day when all of the students received the LEAP Test scores. The date of this was May 6, 2008. I was so excited that I hugged Mr. Allen and thanked him for believing in me. A few days before graduation, I wrote a letter that stated how much I admired Mansura Middle School and many of the people there. Much to my surprise, Mr. Allen read it to everyone at the award's ceremony and presented me with a special award. Upon graduation from Jr. High school, I would not see Mr. Allen until later on that year in December at a local grocery market. It felt so great to see him again after all of that time. I saw him again a year later at a school board meeting where I was being recognized for being an author. He told me that the very same letter that I wrote in eighth grade is on display in the main officer for everyone to see. Mr. Allen has always given me great advice and support, and I thank him with all of my heart for having so much faith in who I am and will become later on. I pray that God will bless not only Mr. Allen Warnersdorfer, but his entire family for the years to come.

During the beginning of my sophomore year, I became great friends with the then-assistant librarian, Ms. Carolyn Johnson. Ms. Carolyn has served as a helper and mentor on my behalf for a few years now. There has been so many times when Ms. Carolyn encouraged me to be the best person I could be in everything I do. She is a very passionate Christian lady and loves God with all of her heart, which I honor and respect to a great extent. We have enjoyed many great conversations concerning faith in Jesus Christ, political affairs, and life in general. There were times when I told her about certain problems I have had that were related to school and other students. Ms. Carolyn is someone who anyone could rely on and be friends with, and she can definitely be trusted with anything and everything you put before her. I will always remember the day she told me of what it says in Joshua 1:9, which has become my favorite quote out of scripture. I apply it in absolutely every single thing I do in my life. I really miss going to her class everyday when I was a student at Avoyelles High. I will also miss Ms, Carolyn's assistant, Ms. Alma. She is also a very nice person and great individual to be friends and fellowship with. I am good friends also with Ms. Carolyn's daughter, Rebecca. I will pray that God continues to bestow His greatness upon Ms. Carolyn Johnson and her entire family, as well as Ms. Alma.

At the beginning of my senior year, I was introduced to the new gym coach, Ms. Jessica Provost. I have always known her better as Coach Provost, while others simply call her Coach P. Coach Provost is definitely one of the best and greatest teachers I have ever had before, and I am honored truly to have had her during my senior year. During the first day of school as she was taking attendance, I was under the impression that she was a mean person, and I felt intimidated somewhat. After a few days, however, I learned that she is the one of the nicest persons anyone could ever meet. It was my first time taking gym class again after two and a half years. All of us were required to wear shorts and a shirt. Because I do not wear shorts, I brought sweatpants. I did not like changing clothes in front of others, so Coach Provost allowed me gladly to change everyday in the bathroom in the gym lobby. She told me one day that I was one of the nicest gentlemen she had ever met before. I really began to enjoy going to her class everyday and talking to her all the time. Gym was a class that I despised normally, but Coach Provost changed that forever. On the day when I was elected the parish 4-H President, I ran to her class directly and gave her the biggest hug I had given ever. I also remember the day when I showed her one of the books I published and she began to cry. There had come a day at school later on during the year when she and I stood close to each other and held hands as I led us in prayer. We were praying because the softball team was experiencing a great deal of hardship and uncertainty. Coach asked me to come out to the softball field later on that day to pray with the rest of the team. I was honored greatly to do so, as this led to further involvement with the softball team. I began to attend their games and practices as I ran errands for the girls, and I considered myself a member of the team. It felt so great to help them rise from hardship and uncertainty and watch as they became strong again. Coach P is not only a wonderful softball coach, but one of my best friends and sister-in-Christ. I pray that God does great things in her life, and I really hope we can see each other again in the near future.

I will always be grateful eternally for my friendship with Steven Batiste. Mr. Batiste and I met on January 18th, 2010 at an event in honor of the birthday of Dr. Martin Luther King, Jr. He complimented me heavily on the speech I gave there, and I had taken some pictures with some of his children. Some of the greatest things I admire about Mr. Batiste are his strong faith in Jesus Christ, his commitment to family and friends, and the great deal of wisdom he has to offer. He and I would run into each other at the grocery store on numerous occasions, and we talk on the phone every now and then. Mr. Batiste advises and encourages me spiritually, which has helped me become a stronger, better person. I can always trust in God that he will never lead me in a negative direction. It is God who is using Mr. Batiste, along with many others, in my life in an effort to transform me over time. I appreciate all for which he has done on my behalf, and I will pray that all of his kids reach the fullness of God's greatness in their lives. I will pray also that Mr. Batiste remains the wonderful person he is and that our friendship will continue to grow and prosper.

For over four years now, I have been great friends with one of the greatest families in the world, the Strohschein family. I became friends first with Michael Strohschein during my seventh grade year of school at Mansura Middle. He was a student in eighth grade. A year later, I met his two sisters, Savanna and Chasity. The following year, I met their mom, Mrs. Nelda Strohschein. I am great friends also with Irene Hess and her Husband, Mr. Johnny Hess, who are relatives of the family. I consider all of them not only great friends, but family. I remember back during the second half of 2008 when Savanna and I would talk on the phone all of the time. I remember buying her a jar of pickles in July of 2008 because they were her favorite. I regret being able to never get them to her, but I promise to buy her some more in the near future. I enjoyed myself heavily at Savanna's going-away party to Germany two and a half years ago. The date of this was July 10, 2010. I love Ms. Nelda with all of my heart as I consider her a second mother to me. I remember the day of my second award's ceremony in high-school when Ms. Nelda gave me the best hug I have ever received. I definitely consider Michael a brother to me, as Savanna and Chasity are the sisters I have never had. I will always consider myself a member of the Strohschein family, and I will pray that God continues to bring about His wonderful blessing in their lives. I love Nelda, Savanna, Chasity, Michael, Irene, and Johnny with every single piece of my entire heart.

I am grateful eternally for one of the greatest friends I have in the entire world, Larry Martin. He is an eighth-grade student at Avoyelles High School and is one of the best students the school has to offer. Larry and I have been friends since the beginning of the year 2012. We talk on the phone with and text each other very often, and we fellowship during the times I go to visit Avoyelles High. I still remember the very expression on his face when I came back to school for the first time since graduation a few months earlier. It felt so wonderful to see everyone again and visit the place that is centered specially in my heart. Larry tells me all the time that I am in all of his prayers and that I will change the world in the future. He is definitely in all of my prayers, and I believe with all of my heart that the Lord has a wonderful plan for his life. I will always consider Larry Martin a very important part of my life, and I will always be there for him and guide him into the future. He is definitely one of my brothers-in-Christ, and I love him very much.

A great friend that means a great deal to me is Kelsey Noel Wiley. Most of her friends refer to her as Kelsey Noel. Kelsey and I became friends through Facebook, but the first time she saw me was during my performance in a school play. She and I never attended the same school; however, I would see her at the school she attended during the times I would go to speak. I was very honored to travel fifteen miles to visit her at the restaurant she works. She is a great person, wonderful to spend time with, and fun to talk to. I have been honored to have helped her through periods of difficulty in her life, and I give full credit to God for sending me to help her in the manners for which I did so. I believe with all of my heart that God has a great plan for Kelsey's future, as He does for everyone's future. I will continue to pray to God that He will bless her with all of the wonderful things He has in store. I have great faith she will achieve the fullness of God's spectacular blessings, and I will be of full assistance in helping it to be acquired by her. I will always be grateful for the wonderful friendship shared between Kelsey Noel and myself, and I will be there for her always no matter what.

I will be forever grateful eternally one of my greatest friends, Dylan Ducote. I can say honestly that Dylan is one of the best friends I could have ever asked for. I am grateful for his family, which I consider part of my own. All of us attend church together every Sunday, and we fellowship on many social occasions. Dylan and I became very good friends on September 30th, 2012 when he invited me to a party at his house. It was very much fun and well worth my time. One of the greatest things I admire about my friend Dylan is that he never tries to be like everyone else and "fit in with the crowd." He loves God with all of his heart, he loves and respects people the way he should, and he has a positive vision for what he enjoys doing. There has been times when I was down or needed simple favors, and Dylan was there for me when no one else was. I thank God for him and his family, and I will always be grateful for everything he has done on my behalf.

I will always admire my former teacher, Merkel Dupuy, with everything I have. Mr. Merkel and I first met in August of 2009 when he became a teacher at Avoyelles High School. He and I were sitting at the same table during lunch and we began to talk. I was honored to participate in the plays he was putting on at our school, and I had a great deal of fun in doing so. I would enjoy going into his class everyday to visit and talk. He has a strong faith in Jesus Christ and loves Him with all of his heart. Mr. Merkel is a man of very much wisdom, and he is a great person to carry on a conversation with and seek for advice. The last time he and I met was on April 18th, 2012, and I pray that we can meet again soon. I will always be grateful for all of the things Mr. Merkel has done for me, and I pray to God for He and I to meet once again.

One person who will always be one of my best friends in the entire Universe is Rebecca Melton. She is one of the greatest girls that I consider very important in my life. We have been close friends since September of 2010. The first time I talked to her was when I asked her to come to the homecoming dance with me. While she agreed to go with me, her mom would not let her go for unknown reasons to my knowledge. We would always talk with one another and visit each other at school, and we began to talk on the phone sometimes. I began to have romantic feelings for her at a certain point. There were things taking place in her life that prevented the both of us from being in a relationship, but my feelings did not fade because of so. The last day I saw her was before she moved to Texas to begin a new start on her life. She asked me the day before if I had fifty dollars to spare her, but I had only forty dollars. She came to my house the next day to receive the money. We stood outside in the pouring rain as I read her a friendship card that I had for three years. After reading it, she began to cry while I held her in my arms. I kissed her on her mouth before she left to go to Texas. I could not stop thinking of her as the day carried out. Rebecca is very beautiful, kind, sweet, and a great person. I will lay down my life so that she could continue living. I really hope to see Rebecca again in the near future. Until then and beyond, I will continue to pray for her and that she lives a happy, wonderful life. I will love Rebecca Melton always with all of my heart and soul.

On November 18, 2009, Lacuna Coil became my favorite metal/rock band of all time. Lacuna Coil is a metal band from Milan, Italy, and their lead singer is Cristina Scabbia. I have loved her voice and the band for over three years, and I received the opportunity to meet all of them at one of their concerts on February 15, 2013. It was one of the greatest moments of my entire life. It felt so wonderful to meet Ms. Scabbia, give her multiple hugs, and take several pictures with her as well as the band. I had to ask over thirty different people until I finally found myself a ride to the concert, which taught me a lesson in persistence. At least I can say I met my favorite rock band, which is something that most people would not be able to say. Listening to their music gives me a great deal of hope, confidence, and optimism for what the future holds in store. There is absolutely no other music band who is able to make me feel the way from that of Lacuna Coil. It was the music of them that brought me into my spiritual uprising in April of 2010. I feel as if they will be my favorite band for many more years to come. I will always love Cristina Scabbia's voice with all of my heart, as well as the rest of those in Lacuna Coil.

Epilogue

First off, I would like to honor graciously the Creator of the Universe for allowing our presence here today. I would like to honor my parents of whom are always there for me, and to each and everyone of you I extend a prestigious thanks. It is always a great honor for me to speak before individuals like all of you in a profound effort to educate and inspire each of you to lead a future of successful achievement. I believe profoundly in the uniqueness and greatness of each individual, no matter what they look like and no matter where they are from. Now, I know some of you are wondering to yourselves "Who is this guy standing before us using all of these big words and fancy phrases?" I am from Chicago, IL. I am currently a senior at one of the best high-schools in the entire nation. After high-school, I plan to attend a top university and earn a PhD in political science, a Bachelor's Degree in speech, and a Juris Doctor in criminal law. After college, I aspire to become a high-school teacher of government and history, then a criminal prosecutor, then a college professor of political science, and then I will pursue a career in politics. I am the author of both *The Advancement of Common Humanity* and *The Call of Destiny: A Liberation from Apathy, Shame, and Failure*. I hold sacred the values of hard work, self-determination, strong character, and individual initiative. It is these principles and values that have always provided the framework for my success, and it is these ideals upon which our country was established. I am honored always to do whatever it takes to help people realize the greatness within themselves. Through writing and public speaking, I seek to make a difference in the lives of other people with the knowledge, wisdom and strength bestowed upon me from Christ.

It was in March of 2009 when I began writing and presenting speeches. As of June of 2009, I had written over a total of nine speeches. It was my oldest brother of whom encouraged me to publish these speeches into a book so that other people could be educated and inspired. My first book, *The Advancement of Common Humanity*, was published on September 2nd, 2009. My second book, *The Call of Destiny: A Liberation from Apathy, Shame, and Failure*, was published on February 10th, 2011. I believe firmly that if you believe in yourself and work as hard as you can to achieve greatness, then there is absolutely nothing in the world that can stand in your way of realizing your dreams. No matter if you are an African-American or

Hispanic, no matter if you belong to a poor family, and no matter what may have happened in your life, all things are possible when you realize the power within yourself as an individual to make the best decisions for your future.

I would like to discuss with each of you today on the importance of viewing yourself as an individual and not labeling and putting yourself as part of a group. For those of you who are not sure what individualism means, it is actually very clear. It simply means to be yourself, think for yourself, and have the courage to be the best person that you could possibly be no matter how others will react. It is also about doing what is right for yourself no matter what race, skin color, religion, or age group you may belong to. I am a teenager who stays at home ninety-five percent of the time, I read and write very often, and I strive to get the best education. Also, I do not present myself the same way as many other teenagers. I do not drink, I do not smoke, I definitely do not do drugs, and I have never been part of a gang. By that same token, some people would consider this weird, awkward, and somewhat strange; however, I take no shame or pity in being the person I am because I choose to be the person who God has created me to be, and the people who object to that will not determine whether or not I will lead a successful life. As I accepted Jesus Christ as my Life, Lord, and Savior, he has bestowed upon me the strength and the courage to be the person He intends for me to be. However, realizing self-potential is not always easy for some people. And I say this because we live in a world that can be extremely cruel and hostile to those who choose to be different from most others. The most important thing for you and I to do is to not give into this type of pressure.

You do not have to put a label on yourself or put yourself as part of a group because many of the same people who choose to drink and smoke and have under age sex and join a gang do so because many others around them choose to do so as well. There are not very many who have the judgment or the courage to just say no, and exemplify the best of who they can be. Just because your fellow peers choose to not work hard and go to school and get an education but instead choose to party most the time, drink, have sex under age, or even drop out of school, it does not call for you to follow them. Problems also exist for those who are homosexual, those who are different, and for those who choose simply to lead a peaceful, successful life. Even while the pressure and temptations in today's world can be heavy, the best thing for each and everyone of us to do is to find the courage within ourselves to lead the best life that will benefit in the long-term, and this is the profound importance in strong individualism. Each of us must take responsibility for our lives, believe in who God made us to be, and hold sacred the principle of personal integrity.

In our effort to be strong, exceptional individuals, we must first assume full responsibility for our lives. We must realize that no other person controls what happens in our lives but us. People like me, your parents, and our teachers can only encourage you to do what is important such as getting an education and setting high standards for yourself, but it is you who will make the final decision to do so. If you choose to work hard and get an education, you will most likely lead a career of financial stability and successful achievement. However, if you choose to enhance all of your focus on partying, drinking, and relationships, you will most likely lead a future of financial uncertainty, hardship and failure. Whatever decision you choose to make, the person who will be affected the most is you, the individual. Life is too important to make our decisions based on the actions of other people, and those who live to please other people rather than doing what is best for themselves will get nowhere in life, no matter what the situation may be. It is you, the individual, who determines what your life will become in five, ten, fifteen, twenty, and thirty years from now. As individuals, each of us must develop the power within each of ourselves to make the best decisions for our future, enhance our strength to be the best persons we can become, and realize the greatness within our hearts.

As we take responsibility for ourselves, so must we believe in ourselves as individuals. Self-assurance is a fundamental ideal that will go a very long way in allowing us to be happy and satisfied in our everyday lives. Without it, we are most likely to be miserable and uncomfortable with who we are as persons. The year 2007 was particularly a very difficult time on my behalf. It was a time when I had very little self-confidence, if any at all. I was wishing constantly that I was a totally different person, and it became so bad to the point where I would not even view my reflection in the mirror. Upon March 1st, 2008, the day of which I accepted Jesus Christ as my Life, Lord, and Savior, I began to not only believe in the greatness within me, but I began to know and love myself. To this day, I believe in myself to the core, and I have too much at stake in my future to succumb to the pressures and somewhat willful ignorance of some in our society.

If we do not believe in ourselves, it can be very likely for us to become how others are or how others would like for us to become. If we do not set major standards for ourselves and carry out the framework for each of our lives, then we are very likely to give into anything that would fail us in the long-term such as drinking, drugs, joining a gang, sex under age, and dropping out of school. This is not who we should become in the future, especially when we see firsthand of each of these destructions. While others may think less of us, we should still aspire to be great people and choose to make the best decisions. No matter what your parents' income may be, no matter what race you may belong to, and no matter what you look like, each of you are individuals with your own mind, your own heart, and your own body with the ability and opportunity to live the most successful, and prosperous life upon your capacity. And if you believe in yourself and set the framework for your life, then nothing or no one can stop you from being the best person that you can possibly be in this world.

In being a strong, self-assured individual, each of you must pledge your life to uphold the sacred ideal of personal integrity. There are many who probably do not fully understand what it truly means to have integrity. Being a person of integrity means doing what is best and right no matter how others will react. If there are a bunch of students promising to skip school on a certain day or skip a certain class, then it is you who have the obligation to stand up, be a leader, go to school, and not go along with everyone else and risk getting in trouble. It also means instead of focusing your life on what seems fun and great, you should go to school and learn and get the best possible education upon your capacity. Integrity is the most fundamental principle that each of us can and should uphold. You can be the most popular, the most good-looking, or even the most successful among many, but if you do not have strong judgment and moral courage, then you probably will not reach as far as you possibly could in life. And I know that doing the right thing can be hard at various times throughout our lives because I once had to make important decisions. You just have to ask yourself, "What will make the biggest difference in the long-term? Which decision will do the most good for the betterment of the future?" Each of us as individuals must find within ourselves the moral strength to do what is best for ourselves no matter what others will think and do, while pledging to always uphold the sacred pledge to do what we know deep within our hearts what is right in contrast to pleasing those who have intentions not for peace and achievement but for pleasure, self-centeredness, and wrong itself.

These are the basic principles of strong individualism; taking responsibility for yourself, realizing the greatness within you, and doing the right thing. There should be nothing more important in our personal lives then upholding these sacred ideals. Our society is broken. The United States of America has moved further and further away from its core foundation within the last two-hundred and thirty-six years of its birth. Decades and decades ago, we did not have kids and teenagers drinking and doing drugs and having sex under age. Society was not a place where those of whom were different from most other people were deemed as crazy or weird or lame people. One of America's fundamental ideals is tolerance: learning to accept all people of all kinds into one society. If you choose to be a person of righteousness and of the truth, that is great. If you are homosexual or bisexual or transgender, there is nothing wrong with you in being this way. If you simply choose to be a student whose major priority is to get the best education and lead a career of successful achievement, then do this with all that you have.

Never be the person who lives to please other people just for the sake of doing so, but reach out to God Himself; for He will give you the courage to be who He created you to be, which is you, the individual. You must listen to the voices that He speaks in your heart. If there is some person or persons trying to change who you are or teasing you on being who you are, then avoid those people and make some real friends. Be the person who sets a better example for those around you, and become a leader in your world. Everyday that I walk this Earth, I am myself. Who am I? A person who cares for people, a person who reaches for greatness, a motivational speaker, an author of two books, and a born-again Christian. Who are you? Will you choose to be the person who lives and anticipates for successful achievement? Will you pledge at this moment to lead a future of peace, dignity, and strength? Be smart, be strong, be yourself.

Thank you! God Bless you! And may God Bless the United States of America!

Be Smart,
Be Strong,
Be Yourself

CPSIA information can be obtained
at www.ICGtesting.com
Printed in the USA
LVHW050320190520
655886LV00003B/129/J